Printed in the United States of America

First Printing, 2022

ISBN: 978-0-9975092-4-3

Rise & Develop Publishing

Email-corey@coreycarolina.com

The North Tulsa Renaissance

Table of Contents

Chapter 1
History

The North Tulsa Renaissance. This book would discuss how North Tulsa went from being a prominent business area to what it has become now, where it is more service-oriented and less involved in economic development. In this book, I will discuss my thoughts on how North Tulsa can come back to prominence. I will discuss how North Tulsa can change its own culture and identity. My family grew up in North Tulsa. North Tulsa has such a stigmatism that I believe is hugely false.

You will find houses boarded up at a higher percentage than houses of East Tulsa, West Tulsa and, South Tulsa. Property values for houses in North Tulsa may be less than the property value of houses in East Tulsa, West Tulsa, and South Tulsa. But why is that? Why can you buy a house for eight thousand dollars in North Tulsa, but you cannot find that it boarded up house in East or South or West Tulsa? Why is that? This book looks to explain that, along with the other questions that people may have about North Tulsa. North Tulsa was once an area where over 600 black-owned businesses were housed. North Tulsa was an area where

The North Tulsa Renaissance

African-American people could have the resources they needed to be successful.

North Tulsa was a business hub in the early 1900s. An area in North Tulsa was Black Wall Street for its booming commerce. The members of Black Wall Street realized that if their needs were going to be met, they had to create their own solutions. The spirit of the entrepreneurs, doctors, educators, public officials, and builders is alive in present-day North Tulsa. The lives of thousands of men, women, and children may have been lost during the massacre called the Tulsa Race massacre, but the slain lineage lives on to this day.

I personally believe North Tulsa has a huge opportunity that is being missed by the residents of North Tulsa as well as members of the communities outside of North Tulsa. Depending on whom you talk to, North Tulsa is almost like its own suburbs, such as Broken Arrow or Jenks. Some people don't consider North Tulsa a part of Tulsa. Which is significantly false. I also believe there's been a systematic approach by some to move development further North but not call it North Tulsa development, but instead calling it downtown development. This book looks to question and identify opportunities, review strengths, weaknesses, and threats of the great area of North Tulsa.

North Tulsa is not only a significant part of American history, but it is also a metaphor for so many communities in America. You can find a North Tulsa in every city in the United States. This book speaks to all of those communities and the surrounding communities that have forgotten about the greatness that is possible in those communities.

Chapter 2

The Railroad Tracks

You don't have to look too far to find a precedent for the American wall that's proposed to be erected on the southern border. A similar wall was created in the early 1900s, not only in Tulsa, OK, but also in other communities across America. This wall was the virtual wall between North and South Tulsa. This wall was erected in the form of railroad tracks. A limited number of people crossed over those railroad tracks to the other side of town. The reason the economic boom for African Americans happened on Black Wall Street was because it had to survive while being cut off from an entire part of the city. There were not able to participate in the economic developments that the entire city was benefiting from, so they had to survive.

When you're backed into a corner when your back is against the wall, you have two options; those options are to either push forward or stay stagnant and die. Leaders of North Tulsa decided to push forward and create their own economic developments. The leaders of North Tulsa decided they would not allow that virtual border to kill their people. The leaders of North Tulsa decided that they had to make do with what they created. The entrepreneurs of North Tulsa

The North Tulsa Renaissance

were like warriors going out to make a kill because they knew they could only eat what they killed. If the entrepreneurs did not create Black Wall Street, their community would have died. If area doctor offices, grocery stores, farmer's markets, and farms had not been created, the people of North Tulsa would've been relegated to a third-world country, but the people of North Tulsa refuse for that to happen. They created, they supported, and they lead initiatives to better the community.

Those railroad tracks did not cut off a civilization; those railroad tracks created a civilization. Today we are able to walk across those railroad tracks or drive across those railroad tracks, not understanding the history behind them, not understanding that virtual wall once kept us away from our white brothers and sisters. You can allow a wall to keep you away, or you can allow that wall to push you to better. In the early 1900s, the community decided to be better. How does that transition into 2019? Those railroad tracks are still there. We no longer have to stay on the northside of the railroad. Our community and our economy are global now. Our opportunities are global now. Our mindset should also be global.

In the early 1900s, when there was development on the South Side of Tulsa, the government was not developing the northside of Tulsa; we dealt with the same reality in 2019. The major developments are in South Tulsa or Downtown Tulsa, which is south of the railroad tracks. A better life expectancy is south of the railroad tracks. Greater home values are south of the railroad tracks, but the heart of North Tulsa is North of the railroad tracks. We must not lose the understanding of how a virtual border or a virtual wall or set of railroad tracks can divide a community.

If you can raise your children south of the railroad tracks, statistically, they're going to get a better education; statistically, they're going to be able to find fresh food, and statistically, they're going to be able to enjoy entertainment and economic developments as long as they continue to live South of those railroad tracks. In the early 1900s, if you wanted to participate in economic development, if you want your children to go to better schools if you wanted your children to see heroes and mentors succeeding, and you were black, you lived on the North Side of the railroad tracks. That says a lot if you take a moment to let that sink into your mind. In order for young black boys and girls to get an education tailored to them succeeding, they had to live on the North Side of the railroad tracks, but that is no longer the case for most of the schools in North Tulsa. You see, until the people of North Tulsa no longer allow mediocrity in their community, as the North Tulsa community in the early 1900s did not allow, the South Tulsa side of the railroad tracks will continue to flourish as a North side of the railroad tracks, will continue to diminish.

On the North Side of the railroad tracks, you must fight for the same things that the people on the South Side of the railroad tracks. The South and Downtown communities are not the enemies, but they have to remember that a strong North Tulsa means a strong Tulsa. If they only focus their developments, specialized projects, and research on the more affluent communities, they will never see a unified Tulsa. We must fight for adequate education for our

The North Tulsa Renaissance

children. We must fight for retail and a booming community. We must fight for infrastructure that would allow a trade to happen throughout our community. We must secure international partnerships, must allow for business partnerships in the community. We must stop the deterioration of our houses in the community and raise the values of those houses. We must get rid of boarded-up houses and refurbish those houses. Homeownership is key to wealth and a better life, so one of the keys to the North Tulsa Renaissance for community members is increasing the homeownership rates for people who live in the community. Boarded-up houses foster an environment for criminal activity, and we must no longer allow that in our community. We were born to stand for something in our community, and that must start for many right now, as there are scores of others who have been standing for something for years.

The North Side of the railroad tracks is just as important as the South Side of the railroad tracks. When you as a community don't treat it that way, you disrespect our ancestors who fought and died to save the North Side of the railroad tracks. It is okay to engage our brothers and sisters on the Sound Side of the railroad track as they have a part to play in the North Tulsa Renaissance. Their willingness to invest, support, engage and strategize with entrepreneurs, organizers, and educators in North Tulsa, is key to our collective success in Tulsa. We are not each other's enemy. We have more in common than we realize.

We can learn from what was not possible in the early 1900s. Investments by Tulsans who live on the South Side of the railroad track is a good investment towards the goal of a sustainable North Tulsa that churns out a 70-75% graduation rate with a 15-20% increase in college and trade school graduates. Partnered with the investments of current and previous North Tulsa residents, increased investments in North Tulsa will save lives and substantially affect the community. Successful investment offers to look for investments from many different types of investors, but in relation to North Tulsa, the right investors who really care about the community are needed. North Tulsa does not need charity; it needs investment, a seat at the decision table, and an awakening that would make our grandparents proud.

We must recognize our needs and foster solutions for the north side of the railroad tracks to come back to prominence. We need to come together and achieve common goals. Attacking each other because of opposing views can no longer be the norm. This community is bigger than our egos. It is worth more than what we have put into it. It's great that we don't agree on everything. That's what makes us American. What is unacceptable is accepting the norm versus what we're supposed to achieve. Our ancestors created something out of nothing. They were not given government subsidies, they were not given handouts that made generations of millionaires, they were given a problem, and they worked to solve it.

Are you ready to resurrect that booming economy in North Tulsa as it was in 1921? I think 100 years is enough time to have let our ancestors down. It's time for them to finally rest in peace, knowing their dream of a better North Tulsa is happening. That was part of my motivation for investing in North Tulsa. That doesn't diminish all the great work the local entrepreneurs, investors, and believers are doing in North Tulsa because, without them, there would be no movement brewing.

The largest massacre to happen to North Tulsa after the 1921 massacre has handed down by the people of North Tulsa. We have killed, stolen from, and terrorized our own people in our own community. We have shown disrespect to our ancestors by sending people who look like us to their early graves. I know we learned from the events where angry mobs of people killed our women, children, and men by doing the same thing to our women, children, and men. When we hate ourselves, we cannot expect others not to do the same. The murders who crossed over to the North Side of the railroad track to kill our brightest treasures need to be remembered for that. Now, what will you be remembered for? What will your cousin be remembered for? Doing the same things that the angry mob did 100 years ago to our community? We need our youth to flourish, not to be terrorized and killed by their peers. Hold our children close and keep them focused on doing right and not repeating the terrorism that was brought down on the community 100 years ago.

Through the small openings between train tracks ran the blood of Americans. Did those Americans die during the massacre for us to 100 years later still be figuring out how to rise above the injustices in America? We broke chains just for our ancestors to die in vain. So, what is our plan to improve our community? It doesn't take one approach, it doesn't take one committee, it takes an excitement shift, it takes a collective vision. Great things happen in North Tulsa every day, but you may not hear about it. Daily, a child is dressing herself to walk to school to try to better her future; daily, a mother and father go to work to better the lives of their children, and daily entrepreneurs open the doors of their offices with the dream to help others and better their community.

Within the lost treasures of the 1921 historical event lie million-dollar dreams, healthcare breakthroughs, and inventions. Within the minds of our current youth in North Tulsa live million-dollar dreams, healthcare breakthroughs, and inventions. Although they killed our dreamers, those dreams can still become a reality by people who are willing to take up the burning torch and run for the gold. Will that person be you? If not you, make sure to support the person(s) you feel can take up the torch, run alongside them, strengthen them, and keep them accountable.

Change agents understand the difficulties, the oppression, the racism, and the marginalization, but they use those challenges as a rallying cry to make themselves better. What will light a fire under you or reignite the fire to pull the best "you" out? You are the change that we are looking for. You are the one who makes the north side of the tracks even better. Don't complain that people are buying land in your community when you can do the same thing, but you sat on the sidelines. Educate yourself, push for change, and see your neighborhood flourish. Collective power, collective positive energy, and collective drive will change a community.

The North Tulsa Renaissance

Chapter 3

Church, Religion, and Development

I am a spiritual man. I believe in Jesus Christ. I believe in his father. I believe that we're of the earth to do amazing things. I believe that it is important to repent for our sins, that it is important to take care of the downtrodden, sick, and also believe that you may have to at some point take the shirt off your back to help your fellow man. North Tulsa is a wonderful place. North Tulsa has a great opportunity that is being wasted. North Tulsa has over 100 churches in a not very large area. You can find a church on almost every corner in North Tulsa. Some churches are small, and some churches are large. You may have some congregations that have a membership of 15, and others may have a membership of 300-500 people.

With churches come nonprofit status, which is fine, but with nonprofit status comes no tax revenue. Tax revenue, say property tax revenue, is very important when it comes to the allocation of funds from the city government. So, if you have an area that is predominately not bringing in significant tax revenue, you are not going to be allocated a much as an area that has significant retail business. The retail businesses pay taxes which increase the dollars that are allocated to those areas. Sales and property taxes are king.

North Tulsa has a unique opportunity. They have great churches, have a great community, and have great pastors, but what I've seen is that some of the churches in North Tulsa are too siloed. Not that it doesn't happen in churches in other parts of Tulsa, but I am just focusing on North Tulsa right now. There are a number of mega-churches in North Tulsa which means they have a membership of 500 members or more. Let's say there are three or four churches with over 500 members. Those 500 members are generally middle-income individuals; some give faithfully to tidying or offerings to the church. You have the smaller congregations with maybe 25-50 members but less than 100. I would say that is the bulk of the churches in North Tulsa. Many of those members give donations to the church as well.

So, what opportunities do the churches in North Tulsa have to affect the community? I want to see the churches work even closer together to pull their resources to help the community in North Tulsa. I would love to see a community church lead transportation service. A number of churches have van they use for picking up their members for church on Wednesdays or Sundays. Could those vans be used during the week to help the elderly get around to the grocery store, doctors' appointments, or help the community members run other needed errands?

I am sure they could find members who would be willing to drive the vans and coordinate that help for the community. I would also love to see a community center lead and operated by the churches in North Tulsa, providing high-quality education and tutoring to students after school. The community center could be open from 7 AM to 7 PM. In this community center, I would like to see community center be able to offer daycare services, job training services, and placement services; the center will need technology such as smart boards, computers, laboratories for medical training where members could gain medical certifications, and services that will educate our children about the importance of college and entrepreneurship.

With all the resources that churches have and the resources that their members have, I'm sure they can find grants and funding for such a great center. I would also love to see a community lead food bank. Let's pull our resources together and have churches deeply involved in leading the food bank. Their members, as well as other members of the community, can help staff the food bank. North Tulsa has a great food bank currently, so maybe they could work with that food bank, create another one, and mirror the success of the first food bank.

It is important to show the community that you are using the dollars they donate and are putting them to work in the community. This gives them visible proof. Since churches and other non-profit organizations pay no tax for the city, which means a limited amount of tax revenue allocation comes to North Tulsa versus South Tulsa, but it not the fault of the churches and non-profit organizations. It is not their responsibility to shoulder the burden of generating tax revenue, but they can be a huge advocate in generating tax revenue for North Tulsa. The voices of the pastor and leaders in churches are very powerful. Imagine if the church and other non-profit organizations working with the city to create a business incubator system that would provide training and funding for local businesses. The businesses that would be created would pay taxes and help build the tax base in North Tulsa.

One limitation with having churches on almost every corner is that North Tulsa is limited on what type of businesses can open. If you cannot open a business that serves alcohol a certain number of feet from a church, it makes it difficult to draw a national restaurant, such as TGI Fridays or another large restaurant chain because they serve alcohol. Some ordinances limit the opportunity for development because of the proximity of churches and alcohol serving companies, but if you have 100 churches in a small area, that makes it difficult.

A difficult decision is going to have to be made in North Tulsa. Either the elected officials and the community must try to get the ordinances changed, or we must take a difficult look at what churches may need to be consolidated in order to make room for the development of the community. Pastors are not going to like this stance, but if they put the community first, they would understand that their church that has had 15 members for 20 years might be able to be served by another church as well. Now I know that even if you have a congregation of 15-20 people, the pastor is still leading those people spiritually, and that pastor feels he or she has an obligation to those members. I also understand that pastors are leaders, and it is difficult for leaders to be led by other leaders sometimes, but if the local government can work on more businesses coming to North Tulsa, it may be work shallow pride and making the best decision for the growing community.

I do not want to sound harsh, and I am not against the church. I am pushing for the development of North Tulsa, and I want the community to see some of the same retail benefits as South Tulsa. If I were a pastor, I am sure I would have a problem with anyone who would suggest that I close my church because, to me, I would think I was chosen to lead others to GOD. Also, as a pastor, my church may be a source of income for my family and me, so I would not want to lose that. Another argument is that if, as a pastor, if you have been leading a church for 15 years and you have only increased your membership from 20 to 30 people, there may be a problem. Maybe a different leader can serve those people, and your church can be rezoned for economic development. Honestly, who am I to tell a pastor that just because he or she doesn't have 500 members, he or she should consolidate their church? I am a concerned member of the Tulsa community who has seen growth in downtown and South Tulsa but not in North Tulsa. I want to work with churches for them to have the voice of a movement of development in North Tulsa.

The difficult decisions that North Tulsa will have to make can lead to movie theaters, bars, and national restaurants coming into the community. It will even allow for local restaurants to expand. The decisions will not be popular by all, but something has to give. Keep the churches but change the ordinances or consolidate the churches to make room for economic development. As leaders, they

The North Tulsa Renaissance

have to make difficult decisions all the time, but this decision can be one of the most difficult of all.

Chapter 4

Where are the Entrepreneurs?

As discussed previously, North Tulsa has been rich with entrepreneurs, scholars, teachers, professors, police officers, and community leaders; so, where all the entrepreneurs now? With the new North Tulsa Renaissance, entrepreneurs are going to be key. Entrepreneurs drive employment. Entrepreneurs drive sales tax revenue; drive new ideas, events, and innovations. But where are they in North Tulsa? I am not talking about the entrepreneur who opens up a mom and pop shop because those are in North Tulsa, and those are needed. Those companies do a great service to the community of North Tulsa. But where are the young, hungry, innovative entrepreneur who wants to utilize technology to solve today's challenges?

How does North Tulsa begin to live smarter? How do North Tulsa residents begin to live longer? Statistics show the residents of North Tulsa have a life expectancy 10 years less than individuals in South Tulsa. So how do we bridge that gap? Entrepreneurs will know that. So, a plan should be to focus on entrepreneurship in young people. Show them the importance of creating a product, a service, or an innovative idea, and the entrepreneurs can lead the innovative change needed in North Tulsa. We must teach our children the importance of patents, copywriting, and trademark laws. We must educate our children through case studies that can show them that their ideas can become a reality.

I am sure hundreds of students and young adults have great ideas about what they would like to create in their life, but they don't know how to do it. They may not know that they need to work with the Oklahoma tax commission when starting their business to ensure they are set up to pay their sales tax for their business, that may not know to consult a patent attorney about their great idea, they may not know that they need to contact a co-packer to package up the next great salsa or wine jelly product. So, we must teach them that.

North Tulsa needs an innovation center that allows the community to fund and support great ideas. We must teach our children how to present a great idea to a group of people and potential look for funding. We must educate them that their idea can be just as important as the next person. We teach them that no matter their financial status, no matter their parental status, and no matter their zip code, they can innovate to change the world. That is education; that is the education that our community needs. Innovation and entrepreneurship will be the key to the North Tulsa Renaissance. We must also teach our children the importance of collaboration with other people. It will be vital to partner with small, medium, and large companies to support the innovation center.

A model for the innovation center is right in Tulsa. There is a company called 36 Degrees North. They are a form of an innovation center. They allow for co-working space, they host entrepreneur events, and they have the backing of other companies that support their efforts. They just opened their second location. I am happy about their success, but they have two innovation centers in downtown Tulsa, and neither is in North Tulsa. Why is that? The rent space for their facility ranges from $900-$2,100 a month. Who does this innovation center really cater to? What type of business can afford $900 in office space? The answer is simple, not many startups or even established businesses in North Tulsa. But that is okay because your goal should not be to strive to be able to pay $900 a month in rent for office space. Your goal should be to create a profitable company. 36 degrees North is a great model to duplicate, and rather than be upset that that innovation center was not placed in North Tulsa, I think it may benefit the community to learn more about the center and look at the opportunity to either partner or seek guidance from 36 degrees North. I am sure they would be more than happy to work with motivated and dedicated members of the community to see an innovation center erected in North Tulsa because many of their supporters are Tulsa and Oklahoma-based. I hope to see this come to fruition for the sake of the community.

With the creation of an innovation center, comes the opportunity to allow students to get involved and utilize their talents to help new and established businesses. Many youths are great at understanding social media platforms. Many are great at coming up with sustainable ideas. Let's cultivate that. Even though the innovation center would be in North Tulsa, it is important to bring others from around the city, state, and the country to experience the center. Allow them to have input in programs and projects. Utilize their resources that many will want to give. The innovation center is not only to serve students but is to serve the entrepreneurship community. I have met so many entrepreneurs who have great ideas but do not know how to get started. I have seen so many opportunities past our community because of a lack of knowledge, preparation of a plan, and a lack of a clear, executable vision. The innovation center will help with that.

It is so important that our youth and adults understand that business is local and can be global. In this globalized economy, our children must learn that they may need someone to help build on their dream, and that person may not be in the same city or even the same country as them. Allow others to help you be great and learn that diversity is important not only in religion, ethnic makeup, or sexual orientation. Allow others who may not look like you to bring new ideas and suggestions that may help increase success. Don't judge someone negatively because of whom they are because you may miss out on finding the best mentor of your lifetime. One of my previous managers told me to always look for the good in people and take notice of that, and do not absorb the negative aspects of a person.

Diversity of ideas, suggestions, and plans are key to success. We must foster entrepreneurship in our young people; we also must not forget our adults who are 40 years old and even older because even at the age of 50, you can become an entrepreneur. You do not have to follow a guide that you must become an entrepreneur when you are 21 years old because that is not the true reality for many people. Many people work a full-time job and strive for their dream of being an entrepreneur by working after hours on their dream. We must not forget the Golden Age of people. These people have been through some of the most difficult times in this country. They know what does and does not work. They may have great ideas but just do not know how to put the idea into motion. Help them innovate. Also, help that hungry 23 to 27-year-old person innovate. Give him or her the resources and training that they need to start great businesses.

Our entrepreneurs can also be helpful in creating plans, organizations, and products that may be beneficial to the local or national government and our planet as a whole. We must also help the small business entrepreneur who has a small store and is trying to make it. We must teach that person and that business how to potentially scale up to a larger business, identify areas in their business that should be streamlined, how they can hire more people, and also how they can find funding that they need to sustain your business.

We must also, unfortunately, tell people that the business idea just may not work for him or it may not be the best idea, and that's okay because if that idea is putting a strain on their lives, it may not be the best idea. Maybe there is another way that you can work smarter and not harder. It is possible to tweak an idea or pivot from a previous idea to a new idea and hit a home run. Technology is a key to the success of a business, and there may be a technology component that is missing from a business that will help improve the organization.

One of the things that I have seen in North Tulsa is a lack of detail in some of the businesses. For example, some of the restaurants have amazing food, but the presentation of their business doesn't match the great food. We must, as a community, be able to have an open conversation with these entrepreneurs in order to help them. It does not look good to just talk badly about a business in our community without allowing that business to know your concerns and give that business an opportunity to get better. We must also not allow for substandard businesses or services in our community. A restaurant may not have the resources of a larger restaurant in South Tulsa, but that should not keep that entrepreneur from striving to make their business look top-notch.

A person may know how to make great catfish, but they are not the best marketer. That is okay because someone in the community has the skills that the entrepreneur needs to get the word out. The best marketer is a happy customer so focus on the experience your customers have when interacting with your business. When a customer walks into a business, they first want to feel welcomed. Next, they want to get a sense that they are going to get great service, including great food; finally, they want to know that the entrepreneur appreciates their business and does not take it for granted.

We must do our part as a community to offer services to our local entrepreneurs. If there is a skill that is possessed by someone, lend that skill to a local entrepreneur. Also, entrepreneurs must look at the vast amount of services that are available online via the world wide web. There are companies such as Fivver.com where you can find individuals from all across the world to help your business. There are graphic artists, proofreaders, video experts, content experts, and web experts who can help take a business to the next level. L tend to want to look at local resources first, but a business can utilize both as I do. The most important tasks are for the entrepreneur to find a way to outsource. If an entrepreneur can allow someone else to complete a needed task, the more time the entrepreneur can focus on success. If there is a need for assistance with organizing daily tasks, I would advise the entrepreneur to reach out to a local high school and see if any students would like to get internship opportunities. If the entrepreneur wants another option, he/she can utilize companies such as Fivver.com to hire a virtual assistant to complete needed tasks. Where you can outsource, outsource, outsource.

It is important to patronize businesses in North Tulsa. I also think it's important to look at the realization that some of those businesses do not function as if they appreciate my business. That is the case with businesses across the globe, but we will focus on North Tulsa for the purposes of this book. Customer service is key, customer loyalty is key, and sometimes all it takes is being friendly, saying thank you, and you're welcome to make a customer feel special. As entrepreneurs, we cannot take advantage of what we consider a "location win." This means that we cannot just think that because we open a business in North Tulsa, people will flock to our location. A location is the key to success, but it is not the only key. You cannot stop with just a great

The North Tulsa Renaissance

location. For example, an entrepreneur cannot think that just because they are the only barbeque, Italian, or Mediterranean restaurant within a three-mile radius that people are going to automatically patronize the business. The location is great for initially attracting customers, but it is not the main factor for sustaining customers. The entrepreneur's service, product, follow up, ease of use, and appreciation sustains customers coming back to their location.

Businesses in North Tulsa must look professional at all times. If the entrepreneur is going to attract the dollars from customers, the business must have a look that makes a customer want to spend their hard-earned money there. The entrepreneur may not have a lot of money, but if you cannot afford a professionally designed sign to represent your company, you should not be in business. Don't allow the substandard presentation of your vision, your passion, and your business. It is important to have professional business cards, which you can get for $9.99. If you can't afford professional business cards, you do not need to be in business. It is important to have high-quality food that isn't frozen and just microwaved. If you can't afford fresh food for your customers, you do not need to be in business. A fresh coat of paint may be $50. If you can't paint and touch up your business, you don't need to be in business. I do not say all of this to discourage entrepreneur, but instead, I say this to encourage entrepreneurs to build their business models around servicing their customers. Entrepreneurship is not for the faint of heart or mind. Neither should be providing products or services to the member of the North Tulsa community.

24

The previous paragraphs focused mostly on restaurants in North Tulsa but now let's talk about organizations/companies as a whole. It is so important that entrepreneurs hire people who believe in their vision. If your family member does not believe in your vision, do not waste your time or your reputation trying to help a family member out. Business is serious and deserves serious employees. There are so many people in the community who would love for an opportunity to learn and demonstrate their knowledge in order to help improve an entrepreneur's business. If an entrepreneur can trust that a family member or friend believes in their vision, by all means, hire that person because, at times, you cannot count on anyone else to have your back but your family and friends. They can also be the downfall of your company, so keep a watchful eye and an entrepreneur, as you should with all employees, vendors, and partners.

As an entrepreneur, it is important to know that it is difficult to find people who will work as hard as you. It is difficult to motivate others to always do their best. It is also hard to motivate an entrepreneur to always do their best. Don't get discouraged if you feel you are working harder than your employees or volunteers because that is entrepreneurship. You should work harder than anyone else in your company because it is your vision, not theirs. You want people to believe in your vision, but it is your vision, not theirs. You can up with the mission statement, you can come up with the ideas to start your own business, and you are ultimately responsible for the success or failure of your business. The employees or volunteers are there to execute your vision. The better job you do getting your employees engaged and excited about your vision, the better off your company will be.

Small businesses in North Tulsa with maybe one or two employees can flourish, and they are flourishing. There are many small businesses that are doing amazing things for the community, and they should be celebrated. I was encouraged to see the spirit of North Tulsa entrepreneurship when I exhibited by Toasted Wine Fruit Spreads at the Taste of North Tulsa last month. There were over 50 local entrepreneurs who were set up with booths selling their vision and passion. You could see the sparkle in their eyes when a potential customer stopped by their booth. My heart was full of joy because the spirit of those who came before us lives in those entrepreneurs. I want to do what I can to continue to foster that spirit for future generations to come.

Our Black Wall Street innovators took entrepreneurship as a way of life. It fed their children, sent their children to school, and allowed them to have financial freedoms. When you have your livelihood wiped out with no way of rebuilding, it can be devastating for generations, as the 1921 race/business massacre was. That event forever changed the lineage of those entrepreneurs. As a community, we must remember that you can kill the body, but you cannot kill the spirit. The spirit of entrepreneurship is alive and well in North Tulsa. We must now focus on education, supporting entrepreneurs, and community engagement.

I want to see our community entrepreneurs not only focus on gaining, regaining, and retaining the customers in North Tulsa, but I want them to also plan to branch out and find customers in downtown, South, and East Tulsa. As entrepreneurs, we tend to get in our silos or comfort zones. Get out of your bubble and try to get business there as well. That will help entrepreneurs diversify, so in case of business is down in North Tulsa for some reason, the entrepreneur may be able to rely on the diversified business, so he/she may not see a significant drop in business.

I patronize because I believe in supporting local businesses. I have received so much support as a small business person, and I have seen how listening to customers can grow a business. I went into a restaurant once because I wanted to patronize it. I didn't feel a sense of excitement when I was there. The staff was sort of friendly, there was no uniform worn by the wait staff, it was cold, and the environment was not inviting. There was nothing in the restaurant that made me want to come back. I hoped the food would be amazing. I took my wife on an anniversary date there. We were disappointed in the food. We sat down to order. We ordered catfish. Once we received our order, we realized the fish was not catfish. Anyone who eats catfish knows it has a unique smell and taste. We let that pass and decided to try the other food on our plate. We looked at the side items and realized the items were store-bought and not fresh. Anyone who knows food can tell store-bought food versus homemade food. We had okra that was frozen and tartar sauce that was store-bought. We were disappointed in our visit because we hoped a small business would have more homemade items.

The service was not the best, nor was it the worst either. The experience was memorable for the wrong reasons. This

The North Tulsa Renaissance

has not happened with two restaurants in North Tulsa. I have experienced bad service and subpar food in South Tulsa as well, so that encounter is not exclusive to North Tulsa, but I hope for more in our community. I do not take this opportunity to bash the restaurants; it is an opportunity for the money-paying customer to voice an opinion. I have had customers who did not have what I consider a wonderful experience with my product, and I am quick to remedy the issue because it is more expensive to try to gain a new customer than to keep a current customer. Those restaurants have lost my business, but I will still support the restaurants that I enjoy in the community. I will also never say never, so I will probably be back to those restaurants to give them another shot. But for a point of context, some restaurants may think it is cheaper to buy retail food and offer it to customers, but the true reality is that the cost is greater than they think. Customers expect great food and environmental experience. If they do not get that, you have lost them. There is no cost savings in losing customers, only revenue losing.

As a business in North Tulsa, you must not take for granted that people will do business with you because you are the only business in the area or because you are a woman-owned or black-owned business. Customers want to feel appreciated and wanted. They want to feel as if they are getting the best of you as a business owner. I remember my great grandparents and how they believed in attention to detail. They were both living during the Black Wall Street days. I feel that back then, business owners appreciated your business and welcomed you to their shop. We must make sure we do the same as modern-day entrepreneurs.

The North Tulsa Renaissance

There are so many businesses in North Tulsa that are doing putting their passion into their business. They are employing members of the community, and they are giving back to the community. There are multimillion-dollar businesses in North Tulsa, but some forget about that because they are not located in the Black Wall Street area. Those businesses still help pay local taxes for our great community. The power of entrepreneurship is strong in North Tulsa. The reason for that is the same as the reason black men and women became entrepreneurs in the early 1900s; there was a need, and there was a person or persons who took a risk to help their community.

The community must control the narrative. We must have a robust conversation about what our entrepreneurial future will look like in North Tulsa for the next generation. We need funding, education, infrastructure, government liaisons, housing improvements, and community involvement to help ensure a continued vibrant North Tulsa. I look for the next Internet millionaires, business leaders, master architects, award-winning physicians, police chief, mayor, and the governor to come from North Tulsa. We need entrepreneurs who want to offer great products and services to the community. We also need consumers who will hold our business community to the same standard or better than they would for businesses outside of their community.

Let's all work together to see how many local businesses we can help make regional, national, and international business. A win for a business in North Tulsa is a win for Tulsa and Oklahoma as a whole. We cannot look for big businesses to come in and save the community. We

The North Tulsa Renaissance

must remember that a majority of big businesses started as community business just trying to make it. We must build, innovate, and support our community businesses and organizations. Let's showcase our local business and highlight the great things they are doing. Together we can become internationally known for not the destruction of Black Wall Street but the resurgence of Black Wall Street for generations to come.

Chapter 5

Community Policing

Community policing is a passion of mine. Since the time of the creation of the authority, there has been conflict between the authority and the community. There has been an abuse of power at all levels of government. Throughout the history of authority, there has been a tax to pay to a higher power. Although throughout history, you have not seen equal representation for the taxation imposed.

An idea for community policing is for each community in Tulsa to have a police officer or a group of police officers who are safety representatives for them. So just like you would go and meet with your representative, you could go meet with your community policing partners. The representatives would be broken up into sections of town. Those sections would be East, South, North, and West. The group of representatives could include a group of four or five police officers who are dedicated to that area. Not that those are the only police officers that will be patrolling, but those are our community policing partners with who the community could build a relationship with.

The North Tulsa Renaissance

The community partners would be responsible for attending community events, whereas they would have an opportunity to meet the community members they are sworn to protect. This will also allow the community partners to make the community feel safe. These opportunities can also be used as efforts to make the community partners more comfortable with the community members.

The police officers would also host events for the community as well. It is important that children and adults see police officers as real human beings and not just a figure to be feared. These events can be as simple as meetings to get to know your police-community partner where information can be shared, and best practices can be discussed. This is currently starting to happen, and I am glad to see that. I attended a couple of the events, and the community members were allowed to ask questions, and the police officers were available to answer the questions. I would like to see this program expanded and more targeted so each community can get to know their protector.

It will be important to showcase the police officers background, where he or she came from, what his or her favorite sports are, what their vision of a safe community entails. This is important for community members to know. The community must work with the police in order for the police to feel safe and provide a safe community environment. Individuals would start to build a better relationship with them, and possibility when there is an issue, a police officer who is familiar with the family could arrive on the scene and assist versus someone who has never been in the community. Of course, the community partner could not be on the scene of every incident, but for the issue that may be able to be de-escalated, a community partner may be called to assist. This may reduce arrests and deaths. For example, if an incident happens at home and the community member has to call the police, the switchboard may be able to dispatch one of the community policing partners who the community member may be familiar with so the caller feels a little more comfortable speaking with them.

The stop snitching movement started because of a lack of trust between the police force and the community. When the community does not feel that the police have their best interest at hand, they will refuse to help them. The police need the community, and the community needs the police. They must work together to ensure our children, seniors, and other community members are protected. I feel a shift in the community where they are tired of seeing their loved ones killed, and the killer is never caught and convicted. It goes beyond police killing; it also includes people murdering other members of the community. Snitching. Stop Snitching issue as much. If people felt that they could truly trust the police, they would be more willing to work with them. Most communities understand that they need the police when they are in danger or something of theirs was stolen, but our youth need to understand that the police are not there to intimidate but to assist.

The fears of intimidation may come from the interactions between police and the community. The officer-related shootings of unarmed African American men have driven a wedge between the community and the police.

The North Tulsa Renaissance

Mainly because there is a sense that regardless of a police officer shooting an unarmed African American, there will be no guilt found on behalf of the officer. There is also no support seen by the community for officers to reach out to heal their pain. To see the police force in lockstep with the community after an officer-related killing is all but impossible, and that is a problem. You can't say you care for the community when you are not with the community in its greatest painful moments. When the community mourns, the police officers should mourn with them.

What do you do with racist police officers and government officials? First, pray for them as they are fueled by an uneducated view of people and America. If the police force knows of bigoted and racists remarks from its members, first of all, there should be not tolerated. Second of all, do not allow them to join the community partners program. Communities of color do not need a bigot in the community. There is a belief that communities should be patrolled by people who look like them, especially in communities that generally have a strained relationship with the police. I feel that there needs to be diversity in not only the police department but also the sheriff's department. Both the police department and the sheriff's department work independently of each other, and their policies are very different. My personal belief is why do they need to be separate. We need one unified public safety force. Our tax dollars should go to individuals who are willing to improve our communities and not intimidators.

The culture of the public safety departments are macho and uninviting. I remember attending a police chat, and no police officer walked up to me to introduce themselves. They were very standoffish and not engaging. I sat back and witnessed their interaction with the community members in the room, and I felt that is a great opportunity to improve the engagement with the community by actually making them feel appreciated and valued. Some of the interactions may be due to the general personality of public safety officers. They are generally serious, apprehensive, and cold. That comes from the type of work they do and their responsibility to serve the community. Personality interaction is a training need for them.

We have seen our fellow friends and family killed at the hands of people who are sworn to protect them. With the increase of social media and electronic devices, we as a community can keep a better eye out for incidents. A vast majority of crimes against the community at the hand of police go without a resolution. We have seen multiple people shot by police for either not complying or even complying. There is a video of men on different occasions complying with what the police ask of them, and they are still shot. The police officers were not convicted.

The police officers who have had a violent past against community members, have killed an unarmed American, or have multiple complaints against them should not be placed into the community partners program. We should also limit rookies as they have not experienced various opportunities to de-escalate situations. The program needs seasoned vets on the police force who have experience in de-escalation. The officers should receive yearly culture sensitivity training, mental illness de-escalation training, no lethal engagement training, and negotiation skills training.

The program should provide a baseline of data related to surveys conducted in the community to gauge community engagement, trust in police, and how safe people feel in the community. The leaders of the program should hold quarterly town hall-style meetings to discuss their progress, give community members an opportunity to speak with their community partners, and educate the community on safety initiatives. This program would benefit all of Tulsa. I live in East Tulsa, and my car has been broken into twice in my neighborhood. There's been a lot of people who had their houses broken into who lives in Broken Arrow or other affluent areas. These communities would love a community partner program.

Being a police officer has to be one of the most difficult jobs. They have to make split-second decisions that are made throughout the day that can affect someone's life. Understanding other cultures are key to a successful police force. Over the past few years, we have seen an uptick in racist confrontations. There has been a view from communities of color that police are racist or have disparaging views of people of color. Those views can cause a police officer to make a decision that is dangerous and potentially deadly. We must educate our police force that not all black and brown people are the same. I know many may say that the police know that. I say to them; you can never know what someone knows unless they have been specifically taught. Our tax dollars should be used to teach our police officers about black and brown people. We are not all the same. We are not all gang members just because we wear a hoodie. We are not guilty just because we do not trust the police enough to communicate with them. We need a robust conversation and hold both the community members and the police officer to a high standard and make sure we are engaging with each other.

Their racial undertones about issues in communities of African-American are sad. In this country, since African-Americans were brought over here in slave ships, there's been an authority figure over them. Those authority figures in slavery times did not see African-Americans as human beings. They saw African-Americans as savage beasts who needed to be tamed. They used African-Americans as chairs to sit on while they had conversations. They used African-Americans as sex tools just to fulfill their wants and desires. They used African-Americans as property. Slave owners who passed away would pass down their slaves to their descendants. So, having a love and respect for authority in slavery times was difficult because that authority smacked you down. That authority kept you from succeeding. That authority looked at you as if you were less of a man. Transform that authority to modern-day policing. I firmly believe that in some police officers in some communities, there is a prejudged view of African-American males.

In the days of slavery, an African-American male was viewed as valuable property. He was also viewed as a danger. Many of the Africans, who were brought over to the United States and other continents, were strong men. Those Africans were purposefully kept from learning how to read, but the slave masters wanted them to learn the language to be able to communicate. They feared if the Africans became knowledgeable, they would be able to revolt. Image how much control over another person's mind you would need in order to suppress hundreds of slaves from taking over a plantation with possibly 5-7 field masters. Knowledge is power, and without the knowledge of what options Africans had in America, they had no power.

In Africa, these men and women were intelligent, proud, innovative, and resourceful, but if you bring them to a country they do not know, speak in a language they do not know, and force them to pray to a God they do not know, how would we expect anything but total mastery of their minds. As I stated, Africans were a proud people. They knew they did not belong in slavery, but they did not know how to get out of the situations they were sold into. Generations after generations were raised in the slavery culture. To some, that was all they knew. Mothers know their sons would grow up to work from morning to evening in a field at zero compensation. A father knew that at any time, the slave master could rape his wife or daughter. No mother or father should ever have to go through that. Africans had to adapt to their new lives, but they never enjoyed that life. Unfortunately, some people on this planet think Africans who were brought to America had a good life. Those people think rape and murder is a good life, I guess.

Modern-day police have a difficult job. Modern-day police should be viewed as authority figures who are there to better a situation, save a person's life, or deescalate an argument. But over the past few years, with small incidents that have been polarizing on a national level, the views on police in many communities are totally different. So many people in poor communities feel that the police suppress them. They feel like the police are unapproachable and that they cannot identify with police officers. Many feel that those police officers don't look like them, so they can't understand their struggle, not knowing that some police officers may have grown up with an absent father, some police officers may have grown up poor, and some police officer may have dealt with some difficulties that are similar to the members of the community.

The community doesn't know that because they do not know the police officers. The police officer doesn't know how similar he or she is to the members of the community because they don't know the members in the community. There are so many police officers that get into that position and lose the true meaning of being a police officer. It's not to stoke fear, it's not to bark orders, and it's not to make someone feel less than human or less important than others. It is also not the community's job to vilify the police.

The police officers' job is to be there for those little boys and little girls who have to deal with a relative dying, it's being there for little boys and little girls who are scared to walk home from school, and it's being there whenever there's a domestic situation in the community. Police are important to the community, and the community cannot overlook that. But the police also cannot overlook the importance of the community. Low to middle-income people are not the only people who have an issue with police; You can be highly educated, earn a great wage, and still have a fear of a police officer because of your interaction with

The North Tulsa Renaissance

them and the past. It is unfortunate that police are not as ingrained into the community as one would hope, and for the North Tulsa Renaissance to be achieved, we must have a thriving relationship with our police officers. We need police officers not only to protect our communities but also our businesses. With the millions of dollars in investment that will be coming to North Tulsa, that investment must be protected. Without a working relationship with our protectors, both the community and the police department lose.

If you or your family members have had bad interactions with the police, don't hold the entire police force at fault. There are systemic issues with the police and sheriff department in Tulsa, and I feel that if they allowed citizens to be involved in interviewing potential police/sheriff officers, the community would feel more engaged with the polices on their streets. As a homeowner in North Tulsa, I want to protect my investment. I want to ensure that drugs are not in the communities where I want to invest my hard-earned money. The families who decide to live in my investment homes deserve a safe community. The police are vital in securing our neighborhoods, but our neighbors have a responsibility as well. Far too long have we allowed our community to be run down by people who do not have its best interests at hand. Far too long have we allowed drugs, violence, and crime to fester in our neighborhoods in North Tulsa. It is time to take a hard-line stance against violators against the common goals of our communities.

We speak about the gentrification of our neighborhoods, but we do not do a good enough job speaking about reverse

40

gentrification, which is ensuring our communities are prosperous and safe. It is investing in our communities but saving our communities from violence, drugs, and danger. Many people have a problem with the police, but the police are not the ones selling drugs in a house down the street, the police are not the ones allowing trash to build upon the street, and the police are not the reason for the lack of support for entrepreneurial efforts in North Tulsa. Until we become intolerant of the destruction of our community, we can expect the investments going into our community to be sustained.

We need more of our children to become police officers so that our community can be even better represented by people who were actually raised in the community they monitor. But we do not only need people who look like the people they protect. We need a community that is willing to fight the reasons for their destruction. Drugs, poverty, lack of stellar education, and an overlooked youth focus are all problems that can be addressed by the wonderful community members. We can work with the police to identify hot spots, danger zones, and problem areas, we can work with the police to patrol our businesses to ensure safety with our investments, we can work with the police to advocate a better community outreach in North Tulsa, and finally, we can voice to the mayor the importance of funding for public safety. We must all work together to ensure that the North Tulsa Renaissance is protected as expected.

As a police officer, the community understands that it is a difficult and split-second decision-making position, but the community should not be feared, marginalized, profiled, talked down to. The community should be celebrated, enjoyed, engaged with, and allowed to be involved. I went to a police outreach event last year, and I felt the police, although informative, were not approachable. I did not feel welcomed. I did sit back and look at the interaction between my white brothers and sisters with the police. They seemed to not have any apprehensions with speaking with the police; they seemed comfortable. Not once did the police officers, even the one African American and one Hispanic, come to my table to welcome me. That was concerning to me. I was not offended, but it did catch my attention. I thought about the great opportunity that the police have for outreach, but they must be approachable. With that said, they are great at their jobs of helping people. A lady locked her keys in the car with her son, and the police officers helped her save her son while I was there. That was amazing. They must use the opportunities that the community gives to be present, listen, engage, shake heads, and look into the eyes of the oppressed, the downtrodden, and the hopeful.

The lack of trust between the North Tulsa community and police did not happen overnight, so the healing process will also take time. The police must show the community the great works that they have completed on behalf of the community, and the community must be open to listen and work with the police to ensure our safety and prosperity. Our children should not grow up with the fear of the police but not with a fear of a known murder or drug dealer who is killing our people at far higher rates than police-involved shootings.

We must give our children an alternative to drugs. We must work with gangs to see how we can utilize their influence to better the community. I just had a conversation with a relative of mine who is a gang member, and we talked about the role of gangs in the North Tulsa community. I let him know that I am not against gangs as a collective group. I said I think the focus of gangs should shift. They are willing to die for land that they do not own. I want to see gang members advocate a better life for their members. Land and homeownership is the key to prosperity, not drugs. Drugs are the key to the destruction of our people, manufactured and distributed by the oppressors of freedom and hope. I discussed with him that if you get locked up for selling poison to your own people, you will not be able to give your lawyer drugs for payment, but it possible that if you have land or real estate that you can leverage that. Drugs generally do not make you rich. Most of the drug dealers are low-level workers. But real estate has created some of the wealthiest people in America. Real estate does not require you to have gone to college, have your father in your life, growing up in South Tulsa, or that you don't have tattoos on your face, hands, or your neck. Real estate creates true freedom; drugs create slavery. I would rather see gang members and drug dealers buying the block versus destroying the block. Gang members are charismatic and influencers; they are able to get others to follow them, so why not follow them to prosperity and not despair. I am a member of a fraternity, and I would never want someone to tell me that I cannot represent my organization, so I would never tell someone they should not represent their affiliation, but when your affiliation has a negative connotation, it is time to re-evaluate the future of your organizations. Drugs, violence, poverty, and low education are not the keys to any organization's future. Change your future by changing your present.

The gun violence culture that America perpetuates has assisted in the destruction of our population. We have made it okay and normal to hear about shooting either by domestic terrorism or domestic violent acts. When a community has members, who feel they must have a gun on them to protect themselves, it is alarming. This is not a North Tulsa issue; this is an American issue. I am pro-gun education and gun ownership, but even more important is the ability to de-escalate situations. We must not handle or conflicts with gun violence; we must be able to talk about our concerns and work to a mutually agreed-upon solution. We are currently seeing school shootings far too frequently in our country, we are currently seeing drive-by shooting far too frequently, our children are being raised in a war zone in some areas in our country. We must teach our children how to identify escalating situations and avoid them or how to resolve the issue. Our children should not think their only way to get someone to recognize or listen to them is by flashing a gun. We have lost too many Americans to gun violence. We should be able to advocate for our youth that hunting is a sport, but it is hard to do that because the vision of black and brown people with guns in American is viewed as a threat to America.

Until police and other authority figures learn that a gun-carrying black and brown person is no more a threat than a gun-carrying white person, their ignorance will continue to show with the unlawful arrests and shooting of black and brown men. A black man who may have the genetic makeup of a 6-foot is not inherently a threat to an officer; he should not be handled more violently than his white counterpart. He is an American and deserves respect. If he is a threat and has threatened an officer, then, by all means, the officer must protect him/herself. Violence, tone, and choice of words all contribute to an escalating situation between an officer and an American. An officer can give orders without yelling, cussing, and demeaning as an initial step. If non-compliance occurs, the tone, words, and actions must change to show more aggression, but punching, tasering, and shooting people who are in handcuffs or who have five officers on his or her back is unacceptable and should be un-American. Unfortunately, too many, that is as American as apple pie. Once again, if non-compliance to clear orders is not adhered to, escalation is necessary, but a taser or other non-lethal force should be used first unless imminent danger to the officer is present.

It is imperative that police understand how imposing their presence can be to those who have seen, hear, and read about oppressive actions and policies the police department/ sheriff department has had in place. Their gun, their badges, their bulletproof vests are intimidating to members of the community at times. I understand the need for them, but at certain times, it is important that the community see the police officers as real people. Interacting with police officers in ways the community enjoys can foster better relations. More police versus firefighters basketball and football games are key, more police versus teacher events are key, and more police versus kids' baseball and soccer games are the key to softening the hard exterior that the police showcase.

The presence of police is key to safety. The community must remember that the appearance of a police officer does not have to mean that something is wrong; it does not have to mean that they are there to harass; they may be there to protect and monitor. If your cousin, who is a known drug dealer, is busted for selling crack, don't blame the police; blame your cousin for selling poison to his own people. Be there for that cousin and ensure that he gets help for the mental illness to think that selling poison to people who look like him or she is okay. Your cousin may think he or she had to sell drugs because that was the only way to make a living, your cousin may feel that he or she is only providing a product to an interested customer, your cousin may truly feel that he or she is only a product of the environment in North Tulsa. Those feelings are, unfortunately, the views of thousands of people in our country. The downtrodden, the hopeless, the poor are not required to lead a hopeless lifestyle. We must show them that hope is key to prosperity. Generational poverty, drug pushing, and hopelessness are cancer that must be addressed daily in our community. We must not create a beautiful section of the community like Jamaica has with their resort community by cutting off the poorer sections of our community like Jamaica has.

A strong police force is a key to the safety of our community. The police must remember that just because someone has a different view than them does not mean they must exert their authority on that person. A free American with the rights to life, liberty, and the pursuit of happiness, may not feel that it is proper to aggressively speak to them or handle them like a roped animal. That free American may want police to speak with them with respect and not an accusatory tone. We are free, but at times, many feel they are still under the thumb of an oppressive regime called the government, police, and sheriff departments. How do we change that as progressive free Americans? We talk. We must be in constant conversation. We must meet weekly or at least monthly with the police. The police should know what is most important to the North Tulsa community, and the community should know what is most important to the police.

The community should know of the police ride-along program, and they should give it a try. If the community wants the police department to know who they are and understand them better, it must make even more effort to be in front of the police. The benefit of getting to know the police is to save lives from unintentional conflicts. My professor once told me that it is important to get to know your professor because if he or she knows you, they will not give you an F. We must get to know the police, so hopefully, they will feel less threatened by the sight of a 6 foot 4-inch black man, a 12-year-old black boy carrying a toy gun, or just a group of young black boys playing in the street. I want an America where my son will not be killed, placed in handcuffs, or detained for no reason. I want my sons to enjoy the same liberties that their relatives fought for in wars as their white brothers.

Police officers understandably are not generally extroverts; they are generally introverted, private people.

The North Tulsa Renaissance

That is fine, but we must all be able to get out of our comfort zone to make progress. It may feel uncomfortable to speak with a police officer, but we must see that police officer as a member of our community. They are Americans just like us. They are fathers and mothers just like us. They worry about paying their cable bills just like us. They fear their communities being dangerous, just like us. We must seek common ground and build on that structure.

Our children are trying to navigate this dangerous world. They need to seek help when needed from our law officers. I would hate for my child to experience a crime against a family member or friend and not feel comfortable speaking to the police to explain what happened. My daughter saw a police officer the other day, and she asked me if he was there to arrest someone. I was sad that she felt that was his purpose. I explained to her that police don't only arrest people, but they also protect people. It is important to have realistic conversations with our children about the concerns we have with police brutality and racial profiling, but we must also let our children know the true purpose of the police, and that is to protect.

As an African American, I want the police to know that they have no reason to fear me. They have no reason to think I am a criminal, and they have no reason to speak to me in a disrespectful tone because I will not do that to them. Mutual respect is key. Police officers should know that all black men do not have an interest in being violent; we don't all pose the immediate threat to their safety; We want to get home safely too, and we want them to get home safely. We want our little boys and little girls to get home safely, just like you want your little boys and little girls to get home safely. This is a partnership, and you have to live up to your end, as do we as a community.

When an officer-involved shooting happens, the community must see the police as remorseful even if lethal force was necessary, but when the officer kills an unarmed person, it is vital that we get the same compassion as they would give if one of their own were killed. We are one of their own because we are all Americans. Police must see it's not us versus them. We all mourn the death, and we need those who are supposed to protect us from mourning with us. I understand they may work with the officer involved in the shooting, but we need them to be there for us. Our mothers mourn, our fathers mourn, and our police officers mourn. We are all people, and we all need each other. If police officers care to be viewed as real people, they must do what real people do, accept their wrongdoings, change their negative ways, and communicate a plan to move the community and departments forward, "together."

If an officer truly feels their life is in danger, I am a proponent of lethal force where needed. Police officers have to make split-second decisions, and they will not always get the decision right. The community may be upset with the decision made, but if the police acknowledged their mistake, that would go a long way with repair the relationship. For a majority of the police-involved shooting of unarmed black men to go without admittance of guilty or prosecution, it leaves communities dejected and lost. Death and danger are a part of the career of a police officer, and that is the same for community members. We experience interactions with those who would want to harm, steal from, and exploit us. Our community understands domestic terrorism, we understand loss, and we understand the hope for a better future. We want everyone to be safe.

The healing of a community when there is a police-involved shooting starts when an incident happens, and you see the police officers praying with the families of the affected. You need to see them marching with the protestors; you must see them advocating for a full investigation and arrest if there is wrongdoing found. Unfortunately, what we see after an incident is the police preparing to treat hurt community members like animals that need to be hoarded. I think instead of standing on the outlining areas with fingers on triggers, the police should engage, join, and listen to the protestors. The police would show more pride in their badge if they did that. We are all Americans, we all understand that police have to make split decisions from time to time, and we understand that there is racial bias in most Americans' minds. We just want to do what we can to help police officers limit their bias due to the type of job they have. I feel that the community would respect the police so much more if they didn't feel as if the police/sheriff's department didn't care about people of color and poor whites.

Police officers need a paradigm shift when it comes to dealing with Americans whose ancestors were brought over to this country in slave ships, whose ancestors fought in wars overseas but were not welcomed home as heroes, whose communities have not committed mass domestic terrorism. Our community feels targeted, our people feel targeted, and our bloodline feels disrespected. Oftentimes, we are viewed as a threat when we want to protect the very country our ancestors built. In order for the police to have the cotton woven into their uniforms, a black man or woman had to farm it, in order for the police officer to have the metals in their badges, weapons, and clothing, a black man or woman had to mine those metals, in order for the technology to be developed to drive the cars they use, a black man or woman had to teach the inventor, and in order for the police officers to turn a light on in their office, or have a phone to answer, Lewis Latimer, black man used his knowledge, his love for his country, and his desire to better our community to invest the carbon filament and help design the initial telephone. Black people are not specifically a threat to this country. We are the fabric that held this country together during wars, depressions, and nation heartaches.

A man who is a 5-foot 8-inch white man and a 6-foot 3-inch black man should not be viewed differently or treated differently when approached by a police officer. An officer should not immediately pull a gun when encountering black men. We are not runaway slaves that you want to either take and lock up for your own profit or give back to the "paper owner". We demand respect for the lives that we have enhanced throughout the history of this country. We were here before the police were established, but we were not involved in creating the police forces, but we should be given a chance to now be at the table and interview police officers who will be serving in our community.

Chapter 6

Gangs Out-Recruit Colleges

G angs out-recruit colleges. North Tulsa is a beautiful place. It is a place where there an amazing middle school called Carver Middle School and an amazing high school called Booker T. Washington High School. North Tulsa has produced a number of millionaires. North Tulsa has produced a number of successful business people. The community has produced excellent teachers, politicians, and police officers. North Tulsa needs more focus on college.

Unfortunately, so many students today see the things that gangs and drugs can provide. They see fast money, nice cars, and beautiful women in today's drug and gang culture. That is what is promoted in today's cultures. To some, it is neither as beautiful nor sexy to have a backpack and walking on a college campus, but I beg to differ. I think it is admirable to walk around campus trying to put something in your mind that will benefit your life. I guess to some, it is sexier to see a guy who use to deal drugs with a rented car, rented girls, and rented money in a music video.

That is what our culture and our community are up against. I love rap music, but I can understand the difference between reality and fakeness. It is not a true reality that all drug dealers end up being rich. It is not a reality that there can be so many drug kingpins selling dope of their grandmother's house or mother's house, and now they become famous rappers to make all this money and wear all of this jewelry. This is our youth's reality due to what they see on television or hear from other people.

Is it now cooler in America to be a dope man than a college graduate? Is it cool to have pounds of marijuana hanging on your wall versus a bachelor's degree? Is it cool for a freshman in the dope game to move up to a sophomore in the dope game, make enough sales to move up to a junior in the dope game, become a senior in the dope game, and then graduate and become a boss in the dope came? Is that more appealing than writing an essay to gain entrance into college, struggling as a freshman to survive your workload, having to work and study and take the test as a freshman and send money home to your mom, who may be working a minimum wage job? You're blessed to be able to make good enough grades to become a sophomore, but as a sophomore, your workload increases school gets more difficult. You still have to work and study, and you are still just making it financially. Now you've survived two years of college and can become a junior. You are now getting into your core graduation courses, which are more challenging. You may find it through your junior year, and you are blessed with even more work, less free time, internships, final projects that determine if you will graduate, and less time to work to make money. Now you have to think about the harsh reality of deciding where to work after graduation so you can start to pay back the student loans that you obtained in order to gain an education that will be used to provide a knowledgeable worker to the great American economy.

Is that more appealing to our youth? It doesn't seem to be. It seems to be more appealing to live in the fake reality of a drug dealer's paradise. With drugs comes addiction; with drugs comes violence; with drugs comes death. With college comes discipline, with college comes excitement, and with college comes the knowledge that allows you to make more legal money than you have ever had.

So, why do I feel that gang members are better recruiters than college recruiters? It starts off because of a *family thing*. Being a gang member is a family thing. I have family members who are gang members, and I love them with all my heart. I guarantee they can recruit someone better than an admissions counselor because they have the passion that is needed to convince someone to join. There're times when your cousin is able to get you into a gang because his cousin was in a game, his brother was in a gang. His brother may have seen the benefit of being in a gang. Do you have an admissions counselor coming to the low-income school elementary, middle, and high school recruiting the best students out of those schools?

I have a firm belief that one of the next great leaders of our country could be poor right now. I have a belief that one of the next great entrepreneurs may be poor right now. I believe that someone who will advance our country with medical innovations may be poor right now. Gang members are able to show potential recruits the benefits of joining their gang. Their ability to tell these recruits how joining their gang will help the life and even save their life going forward. When is the last time you saw your local university representation in a school in your area where there are little poor and middle-income kids?

A lot of parents enjoy putting their children in logoed college clothing but are they putting the reality in their children's minds that they can go to that college and become a graduate from that college. You can also help recruit for that college. That is key to the educational future of our youth. It is more important to attend a college than just wear the college logo.

I respect gangs for their place in American culture. They have tapped into a niche in our youth. The niche of the downtrodden, the forgotten, the poor, the middle income, and the discriminated. In our communities, we need the colleges and universities to come and become *the community*. These colleges need to host job fairs, community events, and college tours. I believe the children as early as an elementary school need to go to college campuses. They need to see that they can do great things, and that is to be the expectation for our youth that they go to college. I know college is not for everyone. But if we set the bar high and give youth support, they may be able to at least try college and enhance their mindset. Because that is what college does, it changes your paradigm, it changes your mindset, and it changes your thinking. We do not know that right now, the future Internet millionaire could be wasting away in the classroom where she doesn't feel challenged.

How do we keep poor and low to middle-income students engaged about college? Some may feel that college is outside of their reach because they cannot afford college. Students may feel that they should not try harder to get good grades because they are poor and poor people do not go to college. It is difficult to show the benefit of college when the student is more worried about having something to eat for dinner. We must show our youth that college or secondary school is the way for them to release themselves from poverty. We must start making college a family thing. If we can get families to support the need for their children to go to college and work together as a community to provide the resources for the children to go to college, we can start a trend where more than just one family member will go to college.

Our local colleges and universities have a unique opportunity to save lives by reaching into these depressed neighborhoods and bring out the future leaders of our country. I have seen in Tulsa, a push to get young people more aware of FASFA, which is a great option for funding for education. We need more awareness to start at the elementary level.

College should show kids if they have a talent, allow the programs offered in college to help enhance the talent. There are so many trades that can be learned at a trade school that can yield students high incomes. That income can be used to help move their family. But why are the local colleges and technical schools not more ingrained in the low to middle-income communities.

Unfortunately, in 2017 there are still far too many people who can say they are the first person in their family to go to college. This country needs as many educated residents as possible. We are competing against other countries in all facets of life, and the more educated our country becomes, the better. With the incarceration rates in our country, we must focus on education and out recruit gang members. We want our students to see the inside of a classroom and not the inside of a jail cell.

Gangs offer safety for many of our youth, and that is the most important thing for those youths. I would love to see more gang members advocate their incarcerated brothers and sisters get high school diplomas and college degrees. Even if they stay in the gang when they get out of jail, why not have an educated gang force. With education, come negotiating skills, long-term thinking, and creative solutions. Gangs will continue to be a part of the fabric of America, and their power and influence may continue to grow. But I am naively hopeful they will put the future of their family members ahead of their gang and put their brothers, sisters, and cousins to seek an education. Gangs have protected communities in the past; we have seen more unity in the years past. I can only pray that we will continue to make progress and all remember that regardless of our affiliations, we need to keep our youth out of prison rather they are in a gang or not.

What do you see more of in your neighborhood, a father and son who went to the same college or a father and a son who were both incarcerated? The sad reality is that when a father goes to jail, so many times, their son or daughter will follow. Now, incarceration becomes the family thing rather than graduating college. We hear stories of poor neighborhoods because of a gateway to prison, and unfortunately, that is true in many communities. The pipeline from school to jail is real. The pipeline from absent fathers to their children becoming jailed is a real thing. The pipeline of educated Americans who end up imprisoned in a real thing. But we can do better. Even if we can increase college attendees from low to middle-income communities by 5%, we will save lives.

I have seen the love that is given from gang members to their other members, and I appreciate that. They came out in large number to help put my cousin to rest, and I will never forget that support they provided by being there. Just because I do not understand their code doesn't mean that I will condemn all gangs because I have seen some do great things for communities.

There are plenty of families who have a lineage of college graduates. They have made that the expectation. Once again, not everyone is meant for college, but everyone is meant to take the opportunity to improve their life by learning something new. We all know so many people who have come from low-income families, but with determination, prayer, and stick-to-itiveness, they graduated college and made a great life for themselves and their families. We have seen individuals go to school for plumbing, electrician, and carpentry, and they are making more money than some college graduates. Education is key.

I would rather hear more of our youth talking about college than memorizing rap lyrics. Our children deserve hope for a better present and future. Our parents are so vital to the success of children. Just because a person becomes a parent at age 15 doesn't mean that parent has to drop out of school. I know someone who fits that description, and she was able to finish her master's degree. She did not give up.

Our colleges are essential to the upward mobility of children. Many mothers, fathers, aunts, and cousins may not be encouraging advocates for college because they are more worried about day-to-day activities. Sending a young adult to college is a partnership between the parents and the institution. Too frequently, a mother has to visit her child at a detention center or jail cell instead of on a college campus. Both campuses are institutions, but we must break the cycle of low income, low education level, and substandard living that makes up the pipeline to prison. It all starts with families pushing their relatives to strive to attend college or a trade school. Next, we must educate the community about resources other than traditional student loans. If we educate the community about scholarships, essay contests, and grants, we may be able to help more youth realize the dream of being college students.

As we speak to our young women, we must tell them the story of the first African-American women to earn a bachelor's degree in our country. Mary Jane Patterson, the daughter of a slave, was a graduate of Oberlin College in 1862. Oberlin College did offer two-year degrees for women, but Mary decided she wanted to change the course of history and push for a four-year degree. If the daughter of an enslaved family can earn a four-year degree, a daughter of a free family can earn a degree as well.

As we speak to our young men, let's discuss Alexander Lucius Twilight, who was the first African-American male to obtain a degree from a college in the United States. It is important to hear the stories of trailblazers before us so we can educate our youth about what is at stake and why they should ensure the gains made for people of color and women do not go unappreciated.

Community and faith leaders must continue to build on their great work by focusing on higher education for their constituents and members. The community needs a sort of watchdog for educational achievement. Monthly or quarterly meetings should be requested with school administration to track progress. A community goal should be established in relation to increased high school graduation, improved standardized testing scores, increased college enrollments, and decreased dropout rates.

Getting youth to become enthusiastic about going to college is a community project. We should have a community initiative to help promote college attendance for young people. We should have college test prep training available to them. We must partner with local and non-local colleges and universities to join our initiative, host college question-and-answer sessions, and offer suggestions on how we can increase attendance in their institutions. This may not be simple, but it will ultimately save lives in our communities. Rather than the North Tulsa community being known for failing school systems, it can be known as a collection of innovative neighborhoods that puts the education of its children at the top of the priority list.

I frequently speak about the importance of going to college or a trade school, but I also understand the importance of graduating from high school. According to the

Tulsa Public Schools, the 2015-2016 school year had these graduation rates:

99.7 percent – Washington

90.4 percent – Rogers

86.0 percent – Edison

75.2 percent – Webster

75.0 percent – Central

70.2 percent – Memorial

66.2 percent – East Central

58.3 percent – McLain

56.1 percent – Hale

38.9 percent – TRAICE

35.0 percent – Tulsa MET

Upon evaluation of one of the lowest-graduating schools, TRAICE, I discovered that its attendance rate is 92 percent, but it has a graduation rate of 38.9 percent. This shows me there is a failure to educate the students who attend. Our community goal should be for schools to graduate 80 percent of their students. TRAICE students are 67 percent African-American and 33 percent Native American. Caucasian and Hispanics do not register a percentage. That is likely because students of those races aren't enrolled, or there are so few that the number does not register. TRAICE is a school in North Tulsa that educates students who require an alternative setting, either because they have been kicked out of another school or there was a specific reason for the departure.

McLain is another North Tulsa school on the list with a low graduation rate. McLain has a long, rich history and an active alumni organization. This school offers a great opportunity for success. It is almost graduating 60 percent of its students. With additional community, parental, and faith-based support, McLain could be graduating 80 percent of its students.

As the community comes together to pledge its assistance, with the goal of increasing graduation rates for North Tulsa schools, the community will see the benefit of using the same type of aid to achieve other solutions. We owe it to our young people. In this effort, gang members can also be vital to the initiative for youth with both their families and their circles of influence. Just because a gang member may not have graduated high school does not mean she or he could not be an advocate for young people in the community to graduate high school. We need everyone in the community.

The North Tulsa Renaissance

Chapter 7

Shots Fired

During this time of racial distress and inequality, we deal with so many issues, but they are the same ones we faced at the turn of the century. This country has dealt with hate, despair, inadequate resources, murder, getting away with murder, justification of murder, and other types of crimes. North Tulsa has problems, but the community itself should address them internally.

In the media over the past few years, we've seen officer-involved shootings, and it seems like that's happening at a higher rate than ever before. But we must understand where we have come from. When we look at the spectacle of public lynchings of African-American families, the rape of African-Americans, and how people were treated – all primarily in the South during the time of slavery – we understand that people who look differently from those in authority are treated differently. How many times have we gone to the funeral of a young black man who was killed by another young black man? How many times have we gone to a funeral of a young black woman or man who died from an overdose of drugs provided by another young black man or woman? Why do citizens kill people who look like us?

Statistically, in America, people kill people who look like themselves at a greater rate than anyone else. That means blacks tend to kill blacks, and whites kill whites.

Why is there so much self-hate in America? Why is there so much gun violence in America? Why are so many people being killed by police officers, and why are so many officers being killed by citizens in America? Finally, why is there so much division when it comes to having sympathy for someone who was killed by a police officer, regardless of why the person was killed? Some people have no empathy when an officer is targeted and killed. I believe if a perpetrator poses a threat to a police officer, lethal force is necessary. I also feel police should use compassion when dealing with those who do not pose an imminent threat. If someone is unarmed and the police need to subdue him or her, a taser or other non-lethal force should be used.

This country needs better de-escalation training from top to bottom in the public safety arena. We teach children how to de-escalate situations so they do not become violent or dangerous, but we put our law enforcement officers in dangerous situations every day. Young black men need to understand how to have a conversation with other young black men, and if there is an altercation, they must know how to resolve it without violence. Young white men need to understand there's a better way to deal with a dispute with another white man without violence. Police must realize there is a better way to deal with someone in the community than with violence.

Violence begets more violence. Police officers should be trained as negotiators so they can learn strategies that are useful in a tense moment. That training is immediately transferrable to a police officer's daily job. The community should also take advantage of the citizen's academy. This would give residents insight into the difficulties of being a police officer. The breakdown in the community is due to both sides not knowing enough about each other.

As a father of boys who will join the group of men who are the most hated in the world, I am concerned about their safety when it comes to interactions both with police and with people who look like them. Black men are the most feared, misunderstood, and hated men in the world. They are hated by other races as well as their own race. The harsh reality of being a black man is that you are stamped as a threat to authority.

I advocate that people not use their race or gender as a reason they are not as successful as they want to be. But it is important to know the challenges they face as well and refuse to allow those challenges to control them. They must meet those challenges head-on and change the narrative about race or gender. As a black man, if you feel people view you as a threat, work extremely hard to engage with as many races and cultures as possible so they can get to know the real you.

I do not want to be feared, and I feel most black men do not want to be feared, either. The only fear I want others to have of me is the fear from a competitor that I will dominate him in certain situations. I want to be able to engage with police officers and other public safety staff so they are aware that people who look like me are not all the same. I am sure the police want to do the same. I think the more we get to know each other as a community, the better our relationships with police and other public safety staff will be.

Police officers have the right to use lethal force. I am a firm believer if you pull a gun or a knife on a police officer, the officer has to do whatever is necessary to protect himself. For the gun advocates who are also police advocates, how can you support common citizens having firepower that can outgun the police officers? I want my police officers to be able to go into situations and know they are not outgunned. If you truly advocate for public safety officers and don't just worry about them when it is convenient to do so, you should support some type of gun control.

No longer in this country should an American be able to stockpile automatic, high-capacity weapons to kill others. Domestic terrorism is a problem in America. We have lost small children, and the very people who were supposed to protect them refuse to do anything to keep other children from being massacred. Statistics show the people whom we are trying to keep out of our country are less likely to kill us than the people who were born here. If I were more likely to be killed by someone who looks like me, why would I advocate discriminating against someone else based on his or her religion or race?

We should protect the police and other citizens by making it difficult for mentally ill people to buy guns. We must require background checks, just as we do when people apply for jobs, and limit the high-capacity killing machines that have been used to slaughter our fellow Americans. We have lost more Americans in our history because of the decisions of other Americans.

The North Tulsa Renaissance

Americans decide to kill one another. They decide to invade other countries, which has led to massive casualties, and Americans allow politicians to continue to ignore the will of the people when it comes to gun control. I want responsible people to be able to own as many guns as they want, but I do not want a mentally ill or a woman beater to own a gun.

We must teach our little black and white boys to understand conflict resolution. If we can curb the violence in our country, we can realize the amazing talents of our youth, who otherwise may have been killed in an argument but instead have learned to deescalate a situation. I would love to see us use more brainpower versus gun power. So many people are scared to have a conversation with someone of another race to try to de-escalate a situation or gain an understanding of the other person. Hate for another person comes from fear and lack of understanding. We have far too many followers in our communities and not enough leaders.

Sports, school activities, and JROTC are the best options for young people to engage with people of different races, religions, and mindsets. We must desegregate our children's lives. When they come home, many of them see people who look just like them in the community. When they go to church, attend birthday parties, and engage in community activities, they see people who look like them. Parents must try to immerse their children in other cultures. The more diverse our communities are, the better enriched our country will become.

Interracial understanding is fundamental to a prosperous community. We must be able to understand people who look like us even more than understanding others who do not look like us. It is difficult to even understand someone of the same, and it takes time and effort to do so. Just because you are the same race as your neighbor does not mean you will understand each other.

I remember watching a video interview of famed civil rights advocate James Baldwin wherein he was having a conversation about the black experience in this country. He talked about the injustices put on black people. He also spoke about the racial divide in this country. Another guest on the show, a white man, had an amazing comment. He stated that racial issues are important to address, but we must also speak about the similarities and celebrate those. He continued by saying he has more in common with a black professor than a white mechanic. While viewing this interaction, I appreciated what I was hearing.

Our similarities should be celebrated more than our differences. As a father, I am going to have similar concerns and issues as a father from another race. Our similarities strengthen us as a nation and as a community. Our differences should be embraced and understood. The main conflict between people is when one or both do not feel understood or that there is no attempt to understand one's point.

Our youth are dealing with similar pressures that previous generations dealt with, but those difficulties are exacerbated with the advent of the Internet and smartphones. Young people are fed more pressure to be violent, whether

The North Tulsa Renaissance

it is through music, video games, or movies. The celebration of drugs, violence, and sex in our culture is problematic. The reduction in conscious rap means children are constantly fed sexually explicit lyrics. The unrealistic drug culture of hip hop is misleading our children into thinking that the only way they can make it is if they have sold drugs in the past. There is no way there could be as many drug lords as are portrayed in today's music, but young adults may not understand this. I am a fan of some music that celebrates the drug culture, but I am also diverse enough to like classical music, R&B, and conscious rap. When you are digesting one form of art, you may not see the difference between it and other forms of art.

If we can diversify our children's minds and experiences, we can set them on a track for success. If we can educate our children to rise above self-hate, our children will excel beyond measure. The pressure of fitting into a certain box has always been difficult for youth. The rise of violence in this country stems from rampant misunderstanding and lack of proper diversity of thought, experience, and belief. If our public safety officers are going to assist a diverse group of people, it is imperative that the officers understand multiple cultures outside of their own.

When it comes to a North Tulsa Renaissance, we will have to engage the youth of the community. They are the present and future if North Tulsa is to excel and become the bright light that Tulsa needs. I recently heard a quote from former President Barack Obama. I am paraphrasing, but he stated that in 20 years, his children will say, "You knew that there was a problem, but you did nothing." He said that is what drives him to serve the public.

The children in North Tulsa need the adults to come forward with action because we all know there is a problem. But what will we do collectively to address the problem? We must no longer accept the status quo. I would like to see a city ordinance that makes it illegal to have a boarded-up house. I would like to work with a group that would go around the North Tulsa community and writes down the addresses of all boarded-up homes. That list would be given to the city government, and officials would send letters to the owners, giving them 90 days to bring the houses to code. If we want to look better, we must demand better. If the owner does not respond or does not update the house, the dwelling becomes the property of the city and will be auctioned off to local community members and investors who will keep the property up to code.

We should work with local colleges and universities to create more bridge programs that allow students to take courses while in high school. The school system should hold monthly sessions with the community to update everyone on the progress of raising the graduation rate to 80 percent in our schools. If there are no consequences for school administrators, there will be no improvement. We must expand our focus on economic development past Black Wall Street. That cannot be the only area of focus. We must create multiple Black Wall Street areas in North Tulsa. To save our youth from the school-to-prison pipeline, we must create a new pipeline of hope for them. What will we do as adults to give our youth hope? Remember, the youth are looking at us to solve the problem we know is present.

Instead of our children loading bullets into guns to get revenge, they should be loading books into their backpacks to avenge the lives that have been lost. Black Wall Street created a system of greatness, and its innovators left a blueprint for other generations to rebuild. We have not taken that blueprint and created greatness. We have allowed our children to kill one another or be killed by those who should protect them, and we have lost our way. Our great-grandparents wanted the world for us, and they were willing to lay their lives down for us to realize our dreams, but we have let them down. It is our time to bring our community into 2019 and demand more from ourselves, our government, our police force, our entrepreneurs, and church leaders. Our children's lives are in our hands. They deserve their community to be improved. Let's do it for them and our ancestors.

Shots fired should be limited in our community. We do not see enough stories wherein a police officer actively de-escalates a situation. More open communication and transparency are needed in police departments across the country. The police are historically private and are generally distant from the community. That is mainly for safety reasons. For years, members of the community have mistrusted police. They have been viewed as only worried about policing the community and not policing the police. We very rarely have the police come to the defense of a community member in an officer-related shooting. Every police officer cannot be innocent, just like not every community member killed is truly looking to hurt a police officer.

Healing starts when community members mourn with slain police officers' families, and the police mourn with families who deal with a loss of life at the hands of a police officer. Imagine the optics and the positivity that would be generated if a group of public officers showed up to pray with families who have a relative killed by a police officer. Also, imagine if communities that are generally skeptical of police showed their support for a slain or injured officer. In many places, this may already happen, but from my experience, it does not, and that is unfortunate.

I have seen a small number of situations wherein the police officers have taken a very violent situation and turned it into a safe situation. I live with a daily fear that a routine traffic stop could end in my life being taken. I live with the daily fear that my sons will be targeted one day for the color of their skin. I live with the fear that asking someone to turn his music down in my neighborhood could escalate into a deadly situation.

America does not have a large number of foreign terrorist events, but its own citizens terrorize America on a daily basis. America is a great country; North Tulsa is a great part of town. What we must understand is that if we are to do better, we must be better across the board. The people who were elected to protect and serve our country must do what they are supposed to do. The communities that are supposed to support the individuals who protect us must do what they are supposed to do as well.

The North Tulsa Renaissance

But we have to all do it together. We need one another more than we think. So often are we on the opposite sides of the fence. I do not believe the police officers systematically want to hunt down African-American men or poor white men. I do not believe police officers want to serve as immigration officers. I do believe the police are disconnected from the community, and the community is so disconnected from the police force. There is so much hate in this country, and it's coming from all different areas. Unfortunately, the adults in the room do not see that this is getting us nowhere.

It is important to understand there are consequences for all actions. If I pull my gun and kill someone who is unarmed, I am more than likely going to be convicted of murder. If a police officer pulls his gun and kills an unarmed person, he or she probably won't be convicted. That is one of the reasons there is a divide between police and the community. Some would say the police officer should be dealt with more harshly because he should have known better since he received training. There are varying views on this topic, but I would prefer to see more understanding between the community and the police.

Enhanced training on de-escalation when dealing with mentally ill people is crucial. This is even more important as individuals are taken off their medications due to government spending cuts. It is possible the police officers will deal with thousands of more people who are erratic due to lack of care. We cannot have those people confronted by police with little to no training. That is a recipe for misunderstanding and danger. Once again, police should be able to use lethal force if their lives are in danger, but we should be able to keep the instances of unarmed people being killed by police at a minimum. The police deserve to get home every night to enjoy their families, just as our community members do. We all want the same thing at the end of the day: to get home to our loved ones. Together we will improve our issues and decrease the shots fired in our communities.

Chapter 8

Beware of Those Who Obstruct Progress

Whenever progress is imminent, or there's an interest in moving forward in the community, there will always be people who will try to obstruct that progress. Beware of those people and the things they say because they'll often say things just to influence your decision to promote progress. They don't want to see progress unless it's their type of progress. They don't want to see new businesses coming to the community unless they approve of those businesses. Unfortunately, they can influence a number of community members to go with the status quo.

The North Tulsa Renaissance is not about the status quo, but rather about progression, entrepreneurship, education, and finding your seat at the table where you belong. It's about leadership, taking care of other people, promoting ideas, and inspiring the youth. It's about bringing North Tulsa back to the promise it was before.

A number of people are set in their ways, and they fear change. They're afraid that companies will come in and take over their community. To a certain extent, they have a right to fear those things, and indeed they should, but they shouldn't allow that fear to prevent them from looking objectively at progress in the community. If you have a problem with an idea, find out more about the business trying to bring that concept to your community. If that idea is diverse and not what you normally expect to see in your community, give it a chance. But hold the owners accountable for improving your community.

Holding someone's feet to the fire is not being an obstructionist. Granted, not all good ideas are right for the community. But if you have land that is not being developed, and it has lain fallow for 10 years, and someone wants to take a chance on your community, give him or her a little leeway. It may be a great opportunity for the youth in your community to see something different instead of an overgrown plot of land. You will also run into political and civic leaders butting heads with one another because they have different views on how the community should move forward. My view is that some ideas are good; they just need to be vetted.

Some ideas can make it, while others may not. And you're not going to get everyone to agree on a way forward for North Tulsa. But as long as you can take steps forward to progress, that's what is most important. If you can bring in more retail, that will generate sales tax dollars, which in turn will go back into the community, which is highly important.

Building a sales tax base is so important to North Tulsa because this area needs the millions of dollars in allocations on which it is now missing out. Some reasons for that are because of the number of tax-exempt organizations in the community; the lack of significant large retail businesses; the low property values due to the nonprofit organizations; and the out-of-town owners of houses who do not take care of their properties, which also affects property values.

North Tulsa needs to move forward, and the elders deserve to see a progressive community booming with businesses, resources, active parks, restaurants, movie theaters, banks, universities, high-value housing, mixed-use properties, sports and recreational facilities, coffee shops, delis, children's party companies, innovation centers focusing on STEM (Science, Technology, Engineering, and Math) learning, and entrepreneurship. I would just suggest to anyone who has a problem with progress or who has a problem with an idea being pushed in North Tulsa, come to the table with an open mind. Bring with you a potential solution, and don't allow your fear to hold the community back.

The community also must protect itself from being overrun by corporate greed. Its residents must understand that not every idea is going to be implemented. Not every idea should be implemented because not all of them will fit the need.

Business is about supply and demand. If there is no demand, there will be no supply. If companies just give you the same product or service over and over again without asking your opinion, you should not support the company. Continue to get behind our small businesses and even large businesses that decide to invest in our community. Let's take our seat at the table and demand that they're going to meet our needs, rather than just tell us what we need.

Chapter 9

Real Estate, Real Estate, Real Estate

T he American Dream for many is to own a home. But many people have not been able to realize the American Dream because they have had to rent a majority of their lives. They don't understand that to build wealth, to build a future, you must own property, not rent or lease it. It's all-important that we teach our children, friends, and families the importance of owning real estate. It is vital to increasing personal wealth to buy a house and own property because the more you own, the more decision-making power you have. No one can kick you out if you own the property.

When you own the property, you can decide whether you want to paint the house, renovate the property, and whom you want to rent the property to build on your personal wealth. I purchased my first house about 10 years ago, and it was difficult to initiate that process because I didn't make a lot of money. But at that point, I was extremely frugal, and I saved enough money to buy my first home, worth $82,500. I had a 30-year mortgage placed on my house. As a first-time homebuyer, I was able to get a loan for

100 percent of the financing, which meant I did not need a down payment. This program is available to many first-time homebuyers.

I chose to go to a bank because I liked its programs. The bank had a lot of avenues for those looking to buy their first homes. At the time when I bought my house, I was working a commission-only job for which I was frequently making just $500 per month. My bills considerably exceeded $500 per month. My rent was $349, my car payment was $197, and my car insurance was $200 per month. So, if there was a time when I got what I considered to be a big check of $1,200 for a month's worth of work, I saved my money. I did not go out and buy flashy things because I did not have the money to do so, and I did not want to let anyone know I was broke.

I lived a frugal lifestyle so I could try to save enough money that I would no longer have to rent a home from someone else.

I initially signed a six-month lease, and after that lease was up, I signed another six-month lease. I told myself that would be the last six-month lease I would sign because I wanted to become a homeowner. I wanted to own something, and I was tired of paying someone else's mortgage.

Tulsa has a unique opportunity for real estate because the houses are affordable. Some are going to need a considerable amount of renovation to get them up to a good living standard, but the prices can fit into most budgets. If you can get into a house, own that house, and make a decision about what you want to do with it, that's what ownership is all about. If you want to rent it to someone else and make a profit, you can put that money into your pocket and save it for future use.

Your goal should be to create avenues in your life that present you with ownership opportunities. The more you own, the more wealth you can accumulate. Homeownership is one of the most efficient ways to create wealth. Just imagine if you can make an additional $300-$500 a month per house. That adds up to an additional $4,800- $6,000 per house annually. That's good money generated while you are asleep when you are on vacation, and even if you miss work because you are sick.

Homeownership is the key to changing the landscape of low- to middle-income communities. The reality is that for the same amount of money people pay in rent, they could be paying down their own mortgages instead of someone else's. A question all people in a community should ask themselves is whether they would rather put money into their own pockets or another person's pocket.

There is no problem with renting initially while saving money for a down payment for your own house. Many houses in the community range from $20,000-$40,000, and although they may require a bit of sweat equity, you may be able to purchase them with little to no money down. There are first-time homebuyer programs that can finance your home between 97 and 100 percent. You would only be responsible for covering your closing cost of $1,500 to $2,000. Why would you not want to own your house for a monthly payment of $300 to $400, especially when rental payments are generally higher, and they bring you no equity? We waste $400 per month just on junk, so why not invest in your future and own, instead of rent, your home?

Credit is one of the most important elements you should have in your life. Your credit score and credit history affect what you do and what buying power you have in many situations. Employers can gain access to your credit, car dealerships can pull your credit, and even insurance companies want to know the current state of your credit.

Focus on paying down debt and paying your bills on time. You do not have to boast a 700-credit score to experience the American Dream of homeownership, but the higher your score is, the more options you will have. Start your ownership journey by checking on your own credit. You can obtain a credit score by reaching out to one of the three credit bureaus: Equifax, Transunion, and Experian. Often this can be done free of charge. Once you know your credit score and credit history, you can start identifying your opportunities to secure financing for a home. If your credit score is not great – 700 or better – don't fret.

The first thing to do when you get your credit report is to make sure all the debt listed on it is actually yours. If you have a common name or share one with a child or parent, it is possible that their debt will accidentally be placed on your report. If you notice that, you should immediately contact the credit bureaus and discuss the steps for challenging the debt so it can be removed from your report.

Next, look for opportunities where your credit balance is 50 percent or more than the credit limit. A portion of your credit score is based on the available debt. For example, if you have a credit limit of $100 and your credit balance is $80, you will want to get that balance below 50 percent, so if you can pay the balance down to at least $45, you will be in good standing.

If you notice that you have balances over 50 percent of the available credit and you do not have the money to pay down all the balances below 50 percent, a trick is to contact the credit card companies to see if they will increase your credit limit. For instance, if you have a credit limit of $100 on a card of $100, but you owe $80, you owe 80 percent of the debt, and you want to get it below 50 percent. If you can persuade the credit card company to increase your credit limit to $200, your $80 balance now becomes 40 percent of the credit limit, and you achieved that without having to pay your debt off.

With good credit, you will be able to get lower interest rates throughout other facets of your life. Wealthy people have access to cheap money, and having good credit is one way to help with that. Bad credit does not have to be detrimental to your plan for homeownership, but you will have to put more money down to purchase a home if you do not have good credit, or you will have to accept a higher interest rate loan.

A number of houses in North Tulsa range in price from $25,000 to $40,000 or $50,000. They have sturdy structures, venerable history and present a great opportunity for you to make money. I have a friend who has a number of houses, and he told me about the importance of owning not only a primary residence but also investment properties. He advocates the notion that as an investor, you can make a great deal of money and leave a financial legacy for your children by owning property. Of course, no more land is being created, so owning land and property is essential for you to become financially successful. You can get into the real estate business without spending a lot of money and without having the best credit, but having good credit always helps.

Real estate is a great opportunity to change the lifestyle of you and your family. Take the opportunity to look at houses in North Tulsa that you may want to own. You will notice the great prospect of diversifying your financial portfolio. Not many investments will pay you 10 to 14 percent. Your bank savings account may pay you .02 percent at the most, so it makes sense to invest smart by purchasing real estate. North Tulsa is primed and ready for you to start owning a piece of the American Dream.

If you are looking to buy a primary residence, and you want to go from being a renter paying the landlord's loan to an owner paying himself back with every installment, investing in real estate is in your future. With a little love and hard work, you can grab your piece of the real estate pie. Even if North Tulsa does not currently have all the resources and amenities you would like, the cost savings of living in that area will outweigh driving a bit further for some services. With the influx of new homebuyers, businesses, developments, retail, and more, buying a house is a dream for so many people, but unfortunately, we allow ourselves to be defeated, and we do not try to become owners. You can

The North Tulsa Renaissance

be self-sustainable and even make real estate your retirement.

As a real estate investor, you may buy one house, get a renter, and make $200-$300 per month. You can put that money in a bank account to save for a rainy day or for when a renter moves out, and you have to go back in and do some renovations. As an owner, you are creating wealth for your family. Your children can learn from you the importance of owning a home rather than renting one. If you want to buy a home and you have previously been renting a house or an apartment, you may not be able to buy the largest house, but it will be yours. You can live there for a few years and fix up the house. By paying your mortgage, you are putting money back into your pocket instead of someone else's pocket.

The people of North Tulsa have a unique opportunity to get into real estate without a lot of money. It's different in areas of South Tulsa, where the average house price is around $100,000. That makes it a little more difficult to get into a house as an investor and actually make money. But you can reap profits as an investor in North Tulsa.

My friend has done just that, and thus he's able to enjoy financial freedom. Because he invested in real estate, he's also able to help so many who are looking for houses. He renovates homes, and he is my mentor. I want to be just like him one day when it comes to real estate. I have been blessed to have now purchased my first and second rental properties. The first property I bought already had a renter. The second home I purchased afforded me the opportunity to put my own touches on the property. I was able to renovate it the way I wanted so it would meet my personal standards. Now, I own six-income properties.

It is important as an investor to think about the bottom dollar and think about providing quality living quarters for our fellow Tulsans. I choose not to cut corners, so I can get quality renters who will feel as if I care about them because I am not trying to put them in a substandard home. I want my houses to feel like their homes. I want to continue to invest in North Tulsa because I see the value in the people, the culture, the history, and the future.

My friend told me the real estate business is all about cash flow and how much money you have because cash is king. There may be opportunities where you get five or six houses, and they're bringing in over $2,000 or $3,000 a month for you. Some people can make more money collecting rent than by working a 9-to-5 job. And you get to make your own decisions about the houses you buy. You can pick the color of the paint, decide what type of flooring you want, and what to replace and what to leave as it stands.

That is the power of real estate. Use your income from your primary job to feed your passion for your second job: real estate. With real estate, you can be the boss. You can be the general contractor, and you can reap the benefits of buying low and selling high. You can teach your children how to be the boss and work for themselves instead of only working for someone else.

Use real estate as an opportunity for growth as a person, too. You may have to start off very small, which is what I am doing. As an owner, you also have to be there for your tenants. If they have an issue, it is your responsibility to address that issue. You will have to decide how to handle the inhabitants who are late with their rent. Do you charge a late fee or let them slide? Remember, your credit card companies do not let you slide, and your mortgage company or apartment complex does not give you a pass. Business is business, and when you start making exceptions for others, you will find yourself in a bind.

As we look at the renaissance of North Tulsa, we need to consider the opportunities for real estate. So many houses are boarded up and just need a little love. With more houses being purchased in North Tulsa, more property taxes are being paid, and taxes equal money for North Tulsa. Many out-of-state investors have purchased houses in North Tulsa and just let them run down because they don't return to check on the house or the renters.

Boarded-up houses bring down the neighborhoods. North Tulsans are a proud people, and they want their areas to look nice. They want the opportunity for progress and prosperity, and they want some of the same amenities as their brothers and sisters on the south side of town. Real estate, commercial development, and retail creation are the keys to a better community.

I wish I had purchased my first rental house at a younger age, but it is never too late to go after your dream of financial freedom. My mentor, Scott Gordon, started this way and has not looked back. He now has over 100 properties. The great equalizer is education, in real estate, and all other aspects of life. We must continue to teach our children about the importance of becoming owners and not just renters. Own your life by owning real estate.

The North Tulsa Renaissance

Chapter 10

The Community of North Tulsa

I grew up in North Tulsa with my great-grandmother, who loved me dearly. My great-grandmother lived the life so many grandmothers and grandfathers live in North Tulsa – and in Tulsa as a whole and in the world as a whole. She wanted the best for her grandchildren and for her community, and she wanted the best for the people of Oklahoma.

My great-grandmother was a tough lady: strong and beautiful, loving and nurturing. She was my second mother, taking me under her wing and baby-sitting me on most weekends because my mother worked 16-hour days. My great-grandmother helped raise me; she helped discipline me and guide me to success. Like so many of our grandmothers and grandfathers, her professional career included taking care of other people. She was a laborer who cleaned houses, washed clothes, and I'm sure she had to suffer through so many threats and difficulties as she grew up in the civil rights era.

Our community in North Tulsa is filled with these wonderful people who have had to work hard all their lives for their children, grandchildren, and great-grandchildren to have better lives. This is no different than any other community in the United States. Grandparents have sacrificed so much so their children, grandchildren, and great-grandchildren down the line could have better lives. We, as grandchildren and children, from time to time, disrespect our grandparents and parents because we do not take advantage of the opportunities they have fought and died for.

My great-grandmother washed the clothes of other people. She did not have a higher level of education, but she provided me more education than any professor has. The knowledge gained by grandparents is endless and is passed down for generations.

There are many people in the community like this, but those outside the community don't realize that or don't want to acknowledge it. North Tulsa is not a gang-ridden area or a ghetto of only poor people. It's not a place where only violent people congregate. North Tulsa is a community of grandmothers and grandfathers, great-grandmothers, and great-grandfathers who worked hard all their lives and want to die knowing their children or grandchildren will have opportunities they never had.

If my great-grandmother only knew how my life is now, she would be extremely proud. Despite every piece of linen she had to wash, she would be proud of every derogatory word she had to hear; her great-grandson has become an entrepreneur and a motivational speaker who is raising his children to be successful. My great-grandmother and many of the great-grandmothers in North Tulsa would wash anyone's clothes, take care of anyone's children, clean anyone's house, just knowing that one day, their grandchildren or children would reap the benefits of their sacrifice and thereby get opportunities they did not take or did not have.

My great-grandmother would have dug ditches all day if that's all she could do to put food on the table for her daughter. My great-grandmother only wanted the best for the rest of her grandchildren and me, and the same is true of all the grandparents of North Tulsa; they just want the best for their community. Their grandparents or parents dealt with so much for there to even be a North Tulsa community. Our grandparents, great-grandparents, and great- great grandparents laid down their lives so their community could be better. It's our job to make sure they did not die in vain.

There are so many low-income or middle-income communities across the country, and many of them get a bad rap. Low-test scores and educational standards, lack of economic excellence and entrepreneurship, a dearth of innovation rule the headlines from those communities. But what outsiders don't understand when they make derogatory comments about a low- or middle-income area is that those are people are living in that community. Those residents have a lineage of others who helped build this country, and they have ancestors who died for this country. The absolute disrespect I hear about our North Tulsa community is deplorable. There are many young people who have such a negative idea about North Tulsa, along with middle-aged people who have a bad perception of it. But they don't understand North Tulsa.

The North Tulsa Renaissance

The ground and the dirt in North Tulsa are infused with the blood of our ancestors, who only wanted a better life for their community. We disrespect them by not holding up our community. When we allow our neighborhoods to be desecrated and disrespected, we have allowed our ancestors to be desecrated as well. Without my great-grandmother, I would not be here. Without so many great-grandmothers and great-grandfathers in this country, none of us would be here.

If you live in North Tulsa or any other community, it is time for you to take your rightful place as a leader, innovator, supporter, star, protector, educator, politician, and public safety officer. The rise of North Tulsa is an American story. The fight for equality, safety, health, wealth, and recognition is woven into the fabric of our country. The most influential American could be growing up in poverty right now. The most inspirational person in a generation could be starving right now. Tulsa as a whole must not turn its back on North Tulsa, because we are their brothers and sisters, whether they want to admit it or not. Our God, our blood, and our love for our country link us.

This American fight can be won just the same as we have won wars on domestic and foreign lands. If poverty were treated with as much fervor as defeating Al Qaeda, it would be stamped out quickly in America. Al Qaeda has killed Americans because those Americans were in a foreign land, defending that land and preventing the fight from coming to American soil. We must not allow the great patriots of our military to be the only ones fighting to save Americans. Poverty has killed more Americans than domestic and foreign terrorists, but we do not treat the battle with the same passion.

As I walk through North Tulsa, I see the dream of my great-grandmother fading, but I refuse to stand on the sidelines any longer. I cannot save the community by myself, but I can do my part to inspire others to strive to revive areas of our community. The local government has memory fatigue when it comes to North Tulsa. It has seen promises come and go from people who say they will develop North Tulsa. Many organizations have given millions of dollars to revitalize North Tulsa, but the problem is that without community involvement, acceptance, and support, those efforts will fail. Also, it sounds good to help North Tulsa, but until words are turned into concrete action, those words do not mean anything. If you cannot move people to action, you are not a leader; you are just a speaker.

North Tulsa could have it all: arts and entertainment; a seat at the table throughout local government; representation from community members in public safety; initiatives that will save our children from generational poverty through higher education and trade programs; business innovation, and more. But we must get away from just talking to actual action. We can no longer just complain about what the white man or the government has done to us. We must take the strength of our ancestors to push us to greatness.

The white man is not responsible for trash being in the yards of our residential houses. He is not at fault for the mother and father breaking up and not joining forces to ensure their children get the best education possible. The white man does not keep you from starting your own business. We can give a million excuses, but while we are making those justifications, millions of dollars of investments are going downtown, along the river, and out south.

Money doesn't give excuses; money only wants to grow and make more money. It does not take just money to improve our community; it also takes a desire to see a better community. If we want to sell a house, we will clean up that house and make sure it looks appealing. We must clean up our community, so it has the best possible outward appearance. That does not require millions of dollars in investment. My mother always told me while growing up that God blesses you with something new if he sees you taking care of what you currently have. We must take care of our community, take care of our veterans and elderly, and prepare for our godly blessings.

I am not naïve to the fact that millions of dollars of investment are needed for a North Tulsa Renaissance, but we do not have to wait for those funds to see a better community. We already have millions of dollars invested in the community members themselves, and it is time they provided a return on that investment. Our tax dollars have educated, fed, housed, and provided health and safety to hundreds of citizens in North Tulsa, and it is imperative that our residents provide millions of dollars in assistance back to the community.

Just because you do not have a job does not mean your opinion does not matter. It does not mean you cannot take the bus or walk to a community meeting to offer your views. Your opinion matters just as much as that of the person with the highest education and the largest bank account. You matter just like your community matters. A wave of change is possible for communities like North Tulsa, but it takes the desire and determination to do better, see better, live better, and educate better.

The American in which all of us are warriors is one to save our children, senior citizens, disabled, and veterans. These people are in every community across America, just as they are in North Tulsa, and they are the forgotten. We do not see political ads targeting these groups, we do not hear town hall meetings focused on their needs, and we do not feel a community push to involve these people in making decisions on moving the community forward. We must not forget while striving for the North Tulsa Renaissance that these people exist and must be valued.

We have the building blocks to be successful. We do not have to reinvent the wheel because our blueprint is clear. We have seen what our people have done in creating Black Wall Streets all over this country. The Black Wall Street has gone from not only being brick and mortar but also occupying space on the Internet. The digital age has become the new Black Wall Street because it has allowed what was mainly local business opportunities of the early 1900s to evolve into a global mammoth of business opportunities.

Black entrepreneurs can now trade with their white brothers and sisters without feeling like they are getting handouts. Black entrepreneurs, artists, and influencers can expand their message to thousands of people outside of the neighborhoods they grew up in as children. The black children can reach millions with videos, tutorials, and messages geared toward helping others. That is the power our ancestors could not even have dreamed about. The Black Wall Street is not dead just because we do not see all of the original buildings; the wealthy generation has just shifted online.

We must not solely focus on getting offices, opening storefronts, and buying inventories. We must learn how to create lean, smart, and profitable ventures. Our businesses no longer need walls to generate success. Our children hold the vessels to their success in their hands daily. The digital conversations that are happening daily have changed lives by allowing the world to learn more, invest more, and profit more.

In this day and age, being a laborer doesn't have to be the only career to which African Americans have access. We now have the choice to become something else. We now can profit greatly off of our labor. We can decide what we are willing to be paid for the work we provide. Our value is created by the knowledge we gain and the skills we obtain. My grandmother could have made more money with her skills today. She could have had other options than washing the clothes of other people, but she was willing to do what she had to in order to ensure generations of her lineage would survive, and I thank her for that.

In this day and age, we can do so much more than our ancestors were able to do. Our ancestors and previous members of North Tulsa built their community on their own from the ground up. Our current community can use the same ground our ancestors walked, built up, and farmed, to create the community we want. The community in the early

1900s did not allow the fear of doing something different to hold them back, and we must not, either. The fear of success is a true fear. It is easier to complain about what we do not have rather than creating what we want.

The walk to becoming free started with a single step. Rebuilding our community starts with each of us taking that first step. When members of the community wanted something, they built it for their community. They did not wait to see if the local government would do it, because it would not have been done. Our ancestors were proud people. We must also be proud of the dirt we walk on. We must respect the ground on which we throw trash and dump chemicals and the ground we do not keep manicured.

We have seen parts of our community be demolished because we did not take care of those areas. Houses have been torn down because they were eyesores. Instead of complaining that downtown is moving North, the community must prop up North Tulsa to be the financial, entertainment, and cultural mecca it once was. Ownership, innovation, entrepreneurship, and support are the key to that. That is how South Tulsa and Downtown Tulsa became the new Tulsa Wall Street locations.

If Black Wall Street had expanded at the levels that it should have, North Tulsa would have seen tremendous growth. But with the burning of dreams came the burning of a future. Even though the dust has settled and the chemical fires have subsided, the burning of generations has continued. We have allowed our dreams to go up in flames at a higher rate than during the Black Wall Street demolishment. Daily, we walk on the bodies of our ancestors, and we do not even say we're sorry for not rebuilding what they died for.

I sat in the room with my great-grandmother's body as it was covered by the hospice nurse. She has completed her race and passed the baton to me to continue the race. She died in North Tulsa, where she invested in real estate, taught her grandson, and spoke about her dreams, hopes, and desires. She died on the soil on which she built her life, and I have to make sure that soil is not ruined. Our ancestors would just sit and cry if they saw what they worked so hard for has crumbled.

There's so much pride in North Tulsa. There's so much to be excited about, and we must celebrate that. But we also must understand the reality North Tulsans deal with. The community faces so many difficulties from lack of excellent education, lack of resources, such as fresh fruit and produce, and lack of technology and innovation. What should we do about that? Do we wait for someone to dangle a carrot in front of us and give something to us?

The answer is that we make it happen ourselves. We use the millions of dollars in resources that we already have. Those resources are the grit, hard work, determination, and stick-to-itiveness that we possess. You do not have to be rich to clean up trash in the neighborhood, cut the grass of the empty lot next to your house, or start a neighborhood watch to ensure that everyone keeps an eye out for drug, gang, and criminal development.

The North Tulsa Renaissance

North Tulsa is viewed as a low- to middle-income community, but the dollars they spend outside the community range in the millions per year. The economic growth in North Tulsa is sent to South Tulsa and Downtown Tulsa, and it is sent to people who do not care about the issues residents are dealing with in North Tulsa. North Tulsa is not only Greenwood; it includes multimillion-dollar facilities that employ hundreds of employees. But what gets lost is how those companies invest back into the resilience of North Tulsa, and its education and security. As the millennials have focused on supporting environmentally and socially responsible companies, North Tulsa must also focus on supporting companies that are concerned with improving their community and that care about the state of their neighborhoods. Although "Shop North" is a great tagline for people to support, they cannot keep the money in North Tulsa if we do not provide the amenities North Tulsans need and want. As we build our own community and start to see even more of a North Tulsa Renaissance, we must think about what the people of North Tulsa really want and need, which is similar to what those in other areas of the city want and need: sustainable resources, walkable neighborhoods, safety, retail, parks, festivals, art galleries, music hubs, fresh and local food.

Building the community back from the ground up may not only be seeing a growth of physical buildings going up, but it may be a growth of moving toward a change. A change in mindset is essential, and it is the catalyst of growth needed in North Tulsa.

The North Tulsa Renaissance

The North Tulsa Renaissance is all about the future while remembering the past. I don't want my great-grandmother to look down on me and be disappointed. We must build up our community while focusing on and respecting the past. An African-American woman no longer has to wash another person's clothes to make a living. She can now own a company that employs others to wash those clothes. Love you, Nanny.

Chapter 11

Self-Improvement

As we look at what the North Tulsa community needs, we must look internally to see what we are willing to give up to see a renaissance. Great things are usually not accomplished without breaking down or tearing down something first to build up greatness. It's the same philosophy as breaking down your muscles while you're working out to build up your strength and muscle mass. It's the same as clearing out a grove of trees to build up a business.

To get North Tulsa back to the prominence where it belongs, some things are going to have to change; they can no longer be status quo. The current businesses in North Tulsa and the current mindset of individuals there, as well as the political climate in Tulsa, must change. Chance unlocks the door to greatness.

What are you willing to give up to achieve a North Tulsa renaissance? Changing that perception of North Tulsa in the city as a whole must start with North Tulsans. They must show the world who they really are. North Tulsa must succeed and prosper, and it must self-police itself.

The North Tulsa Renaissance

How do we do that? We ensure that our community is clean by organizing cleanup efforts. I see them going on from time to time, and I applaud those efforts. We must continue these projects. We need to find ways to help the elderly by cutting their grass, doing housework, or running errands for them. We can do the same for disabled members of the community. We should also identify boarded-up houses and work with the city to see what options we have to secure funds to have those renovated.

We must hold our education system to a higher standard. First, we must allow additional time for parents and other volunteers to go into the schools and help the teachers and administrators. We need to ensure they are focusing on moving our kids up to the next level and not just maintaining the status quo. It must no longer be tolerable for the schools in North Tulsa to fail. They cannot be allowed to have a below-average graduation rate. We must look at the statistics and hold our administrators, teachers, and politicians accountable for those numbers.

Our community and children deserve a renaissance of epic proportions, but will it happen in our lifetime? We must hold people accountable who tear up our community. If someone wants to go on a robbery spree or intimidate people, we must identify the perpetrators and get them out of the community. That may be your cousin, your uncle, or your aunt, but someone is going to have to talk to those people and let them know that if we don't build up our own community, no one else will respect it. If we don't speak out about the injustices we have within our community, no one else is going to respect us. The things we allow in North

Tulsa would never be allowed in South Tulsa because those residents would not stand for it.

When we are complaining about the current state of North Tulsa, we must look at why people are not in a rush to invest in our community. It's because of the viewpoint of the people in North Tulsa. The residents are marketed not as loving, passionate, hard-working people but as people who are violent, thieves, gang members, and people who are reliant on the government. An effective marketing campaign is ongoing daily by the media outlets, our co-workers, teachers, public safety officers, and even people within the North Tulsa community to perpetuate the stereotypes that regress our development.

It's true that North Tulsa does have violence, poverty, and overuse of government assistance, crime, drugs, and more negative aspects. But there are scores more people who are not involved in those negative activities. It's the small minority of traitors to the pure fabric – the ancestors of North Tulsa – who are causing the community to be labeled in a negative way. What will you do to help stop that? That question is essential to begin realizing a North Tulsa Renaissance.

How has development in small towns such as Owasso been realized? Owasso is only minutes from North Tulsa, but the communities could not be further apart in terms of development. Owasso is considered by some as a suburb of Tulsa, but it is managed separately. It has its own government and community leaders. Owasso was mainly vacant land until massive amounts of development started years ago. That development brought in new home buyers and regenerated the high school sports programs, which won championships in football and girls' basketball a couple of years ago.

Why do we see signs daily from companies announcing they are locating operations in Owasso? How did a relative small-town blossom into an investment paradise? According to a Tulsa World article in 2007, the reason for the emphasized investment is due to the community's emphasis on excellent education, solid infrastructure, a progressive business environment, and quality of life. The article goes on to detail the investments in school building structures, the supportive entrepreneur climate, and the access to quality health care. News on 6 online articles in 2004 discussed the farmland that was being turned into a $50 million shopping center. North Tulsa has acres of land ready for development, but what is keeping investors away?

We frequently communicate that North Tulsa residents must create things they want by themselves, but just as the Black Wall Street entrepreneurs faced challenges, the current residents of North Tulsa are hindered by the fact that the government is not built to truly help them achieve success. Is that intentional on the part of the Tulsa government, or is it because of the lack of awareness of programs, grants, investment options, and tax incentives offered by the local and federal government? My personal view is that it is a bit of both.

The government is provided millions of federal dollars to help its citizens, but the residents of North Tulsa feel slighted each budget year. The schools are failing the students. The entrepreneurial segment is trying its best to invest in the community, but it needs additional investment, guidance, and support. The North Tulsa community would love to welcome national investments from companies such as Walmart, Lowe's, Best Buy, etc. If your first thought when you read the names of these corporations was that the community would rob them blind if they invested in North Tulsa, it just proves we have a long way to go.

The buying power of the "black dollar" was relevant during the creation of Black Wall Street, but that currency is no longer heavily realized in the North Tulsa community. The black dollar now leaves us without investment in our own community. The black dollar accounts for $1.3 trillion to $1.5 trillion in buying power, but according to Phillip Jackson, founder, and chairman of the Black Star Project, only $26 billion is circulated in the black community. One of the most woke hip-hop legends, Nas, stated in his song, "Nas Album Done," that "we get government aid and spend it at they stores putting their kids through college, we need balance so we can lease and own deeds in our projects." This is especially telling because, with the globalization of the black dollar, we tend to forget the importance of investing in our own.

This is not intended to guilt anyone, which seems to happen too often in black communities. I would prefer to show the opportunities available, the history that can be made, the lives that could be saved, and the ownership that can be realized at a relatively low investment. If the black dollar were a country, it would be the 14th or 15th largest country in the world. Let that sink in.

The North Tulsa Renaissance

The Hispanic dollar is right behind the black dollar, with over $1 billion in buying power, but Latinos invest more into their communities than blacks do into the development of their communities. Has the black community fallen behind in creating entrepreneurs and been dwarfed by the Hispanic entrepreneurs? Hispanic Americans did not go through years of slavery, and most were able to come to this country because they chose to be here. Many of them see America as a promised land, while many black people see America as a regressive, racist, sexist, homophobic country. But we must remember that as black people, we helped build this country and create the generations of wealth that are still being passed down by many initial slave owners. We cared for some of the most influential and polarized people in history by administering medical care to them, raising their children, and protecting their families, and we have built our buying power from essentially zero to the 15th largest country.

I am not opposed to spending money with non-black entrepreneurs, but I do think the channel out of poverty is entrepreneurship, which must garner support in the community. How can North Tulsa entrepreneurs not only gain support from their community but from others on various sides of town? What does a North Tulsa entrepreneur offer a South Tulsa consumer that he or she cannot get in South Tulsa or Downtown? That is the key to effective entrepreneurship: What demand can your service fill?

A friend of mine recently told me that for a company in North Tulsa to draw financial support from Tulsa as a whole, it would have to create more destination opportunities. In other words, what does your business offer that is so unique it will draw people from 50 miles to support it? Do you offer amazing service, or have a shop that sells one-of-a-kind gifts, and can you meet the demand of customers?

Another issue is that North Tulsa entrepreneurs must think about the changing customers who prefer to order online, support more socially responsible businesses, and want quick service. It may be difficult to initially convince South Tulsa, East Tulsa, and West Tulsa consumers to travel to North Tulsa for various reasons, but you may be able to persuade them to visit your online store to support you that way. Support is support, whether at your brick-and-mortar store or online.

The same philosophies that made affluent communities prosper in the past hold true today, and the same thinking that has kept North Tulsa from realizing its true renaissance is still self-evident today. North Tulsa is exceptional in so many ways, and we must harness the entrepreneurial spirit that was left for us. The renaissance is not a one-person job; it will take thousands of people and millions of dollars. To affluent neighbors, that means a couple months of planning. Unfortunately, North Tulsa has suffered through 100 years of missed opportunities. But that trend is changing drastically, thanks to the great people in the community.

We have to get back to what we did to make North Tulsa so exceptional. I know many people believe segregation helped black people in Tulsa in the past, but we live in a global world, and we must teach our children about the importance of thinking globally and not just locally. We have to get our children out of the community, so they'll recognize that everything does not revolve around one small area because there is a vast world out there. We should want our children to go to great schools within the state of Oklahoma or even outside of the state so they can bring back the knowledge and new ideas about technology and innovations to our community. We must do everything we can to get our young adults to college because as they succeed, the community succeeds.

It's essential that the community take control of its future. Its people must take ownership of the community as a whole. Collaborating with other areas in the city is critical to forging partnerships, pooling resources, and undertaking joint ventures. There is no reason for North Tulsa to reinvent the wheel when it comes to changing the community because there are templates of success we can follow.

We are seeing a couple of investments in North Tulsa, such as QuikTrip and Amazon. These announcements are touted as wins for North Tulsa, and they are, but I wonder if there was a concerted effort by Tulsa to negotiate for at least 10 to 20 percent of the workforce being hired directly from North Tulsa? Those kinds of agreements on behalf of a community are needed from our Tulsa government. The community needs not only government leadership but also community leadership to strive for the best North Tulsa that we all imagine.

Chapter 12

Support, Support, Support

Support is vital for the resurgence of North Tulsa. It should come from people outside of North Tulsa, as well as those within the community. Without support, the revolution will not be televised, and it could cease to exist. So many other communities have support within their own neighborhoods, and the people provide economic stimulus by shopping and engaging with their communities. If a community is to rise out of the ashes and rebuild, it must have the support of everyone and the resilience of a champion. The entrepreneurs on Black Wall Street in the early 1900\s revealed the road map the entrepreneurs of 2019 and beyond should follow. We must build what we had before the massacre event and what we had afterward. If the community has not rebuilt to the levels of almost 100 years ago, there is a problem. But there is also an opportunity.

The community will support what its people deem to be filling a need. One of the largest industries in the country is the service industry. North Tulsa is full of resource services, such as those that help pay for childcare, groceries, utility bills, and housing. But North Tulsa lacks an abundance of economic services, such as a variety of restaurants, wine bars, tattoo shops, hotels, retail groceries, breweries, kids' party centers, bowling alleys, movie theaters, and more.

Without support, the North Tulsa Renaissance cannot survive. So, we must garner support from community leaders, faith-based leaders, organizational leaders, and our community as a whole. We also must realize that with support comes criticism. It is important to understand that blind support is not beneficial to the North Tulsa Renaissance. It is fine to have differences of opinion, but civility in disagreement is key to mutually beneficial situations.

You can support a plan, an idea, or a theory, but you may not support every aspect of it. But criticism is healthy, and if you want to open a new business in North Tulsa, you have to understand that. People should be able to criticize your plans, but that analysis should come from the heart in trying to improve the community rather than a malicious attack. Constructive criticism should not tear down a person's dream but help build a solid foundation for future growth and development.

What will improve the lives of those living in low- to middle-income communities are the same thing that worked almost 100 years ago, and that is entrepreneurship and support. What divides a community is not feeling connected to the entrepreneurs or not sharing their vision. That causes animosity from time to time, which is unhealthy. If we want investment in our community, it is vital that we understand what comes with investment. With investment comes growth, tax revenue for schools, and improved health outcomes. With disinvestment comes generations of poverty, low graduation rates, and decreased health outcomes.

North Tulsa must be open for business. The youth need a future, and the current members of the community must ensure their survival in this competitive world. The community should support the dreams of our youth so the young people will keep coming back with their innovations, creations, and investments.

The youth are not the only important aspect of the community, as great ideas come from the minds of people who are 40, 50, 60, and older. Many of them lack funding, planning, and resources to make their dreams a reality. Having an avenue to help these innovative thinkers is paramount to realizing the great people resources North Tulsa has.

When you look at the huge buildings in Downtown Tulsa, the beautiful new real estate in South Tulsa, and some renewed development in West Tulsa, all those plans started with someone willing to take a chance on an entrepreneur, developer, or innovator. With the negative stigma placed on North Tulsa, investors are reluctant to invest due to fear of losing their money. We as a community must temper those fears by crowdfunding to raise capital for development, entrepreneurial efforts, and community beautification. If we can limit the risks of development by applying for grants, allowing the community to invest, and partnering with existing businesses and organizations to help plan and implement new projects, we will see increased funding in our community.

The North Tulsa Renaissance

Investors want to see that the community has some skin in the game. If Black Wall Street had not initially been destroyed and had survived for generations as designed, we would have seen huge investments into growing that area and hundreds of millionaires created. Just imagine what would have happened if the entrepreneurs and ancestors of Black Wall Street had created a joint business they could have taken public on the stock market. Think about all the lives that would have been changed.

These cans still happen. Let's help our community businesses flourish and create generational wealth. With local investments will come a renewed interest in creating multiple Black Wall Street areas – not by name, but by the mission to create, build, and support – in North Tulsa. We can build off the current and past entrepreneurs on Black Wall Street and shore up other areas of North Tulsa while still showing respect and love and supporting the original Black Wall Street.

As a community, we must create beautiful new buildings and renovate old buildings into appealing works of art that house creativity, innovation, and financial independence. We must create destinations and memorable monuments that will bring Oklahomans from all over the state to witness greatness. North Tulsa is land-rich and investment-poor. If millions of dollars were pumped into North Tulsa as in other communities, the area would flourish. Let's not complain that we don't have something when we have not provided the plan for execution. Let's take action on the dreams many entrepreneurs have and help them rise about the fray.

The North Tulsa Renaissance

The North Tulsa community, just like other communities, will have those who oppose anything they did not come up with, or that did not originate within their circle of friends. Be wary of those people, but do not allow them to knock you off your podium. You are meant for greatness, and if someone didn't have a problem with your trying to benefit the community, you would not be doing something right. Statues are not built for haters, monuments are not erected to honor those who have a short vision of resurgence, and no single plan will bring prosperity back to North Tulsa. If all our young people see our community leaders, political supporters, and activists bashing the dreams of local entrepreneurs, they will be less likely to return to Tulsa after they complete their education.

North Tulsa needs new patriots, and if we do not encourage pride, ownership, support, and prosperity, we will lose our youth to other states. This is not the youth's fault but the fault of the current community of naysayers. There are elderly activists who are fighting until their last breath to realize a North Tulsa Renaissance. Without their love for the community and their refusal to live with the status quo, our community would be worse off. I thank them for their dedication and try daily to make them proud and improve our community, as do so many other people.

A community is only as good as the people who are living there. We must all support a better North Tulsa. We must find a way to employ the poor and decrease generational poverty and substandard education. The dreams of our Black Wall Street ancestors can be realized in our generation with the collective support of Tulsa. Let's cultivate proposals, plans, and financing opportunities, land availability, and make our dreams come true. The future millionaires are currently sitting in the community with a million-dollar idea or plan. We need to tap into the potential of our richest resource, our people.

North Tulsa needs community business incubator systems to allow for the growth and expansion of ideas. The dream of making Tulsa the best city possible includes making North Tulsa the best community it can be. We must help support our own community. The people who used to live here must never forget their roots and try, as they are able to give back to the community. But the community must have something for them to give back to.

North Tulsa vibrancy depends on support. Government, local business, and local university support are key to changing the landscape of North Tulsa to support its worthy inhabitants. Deep ties to success must be remembered and strengthened. There are too many great ideas, great people, and great experiences not to realize the North Tulsa Renaissance.

Chapter 13

As a Renaissance Starts, Continued Support is Needed

As funding and ideas start rolling into North Tulsa, members of the community must support new projects. They must get involved to find out what is being proposed. They must have an opportunity to voice their suggestions, concerns, and ideas for what's coming into their community. We will see increased developments once the North Tulsa Renaissance starts. We'll see new housing, new businesses, and new opportunities for large companies to come in for investment. Businesses come into a community because they see a benefit in being there. Let's take care of those investments and appreciate them because those investments absorb the risk from the people who are trying to bring the renaissance to North Tulsa.

So many times in communities where civil unrest may happen, you see riots break out, and people tear up their own communities. I'm proud to say that Tulsa is not like that. We've had many injustices, but we don't tear up our own neighborhoods. So, we must support the things that are happening in our community. We must spread the word about meetings, activities, and events that showcase the new things happening in North Tulsa. When new businesses pop up, we must patronize them so they can thrive and be successful because that's what happens on other sides of the town. If a business is not viable, it will fail – just like a business would fail in South, East, or West Tulsa.

If the North Tulsa Renaissance is to be realized, we must do everything we can to help those businesses succeed. By the same token, owners of those businesses must reach out to the community and let its residents know they are there and that they want their support. Businesses or organizations can't just take anyone for granted. They can't expect people to support them simply because they are black-owned or because they invested in North Tulsa. It doesn't work that way. The community members are not robots. They're amazing people who come from a lineage of inventors, teachers, business people, and politicians. So, a businessperson coming into North Tulsa cannot take that for granted because those people are intelligent, and they will sniff out any inaccuracies or misleading information, and they will not support that business.

It will take the entire community to realize the North Tulsa Renaissance. Their dollars will help dictate if a business is going to survive. And as the investment comes into North Tulsa, fear will set in as well. One reason that will happen is that even though North Tulsa is not up to the level where it used to be, some people have become complacent with being overlooked. They've become skeptical of why new people would come in to invest or build in their community. They may be nervous that an entrepreneur will come in and take the land that used to be owned by members of their family or the community.

That fear is warranted. There is nothing wrong with looking at investments or developments with tempered skepticism. But that's why it's so important for anyone investing in North Tulsa to reach out to the community members and show them their plan so the people can support or potentially critique that plan to make it better. Plans, ideas, and development must be tailored to the community, but there will also be a need to spur development that is not normally available in the area. Not only do we want to bring community members to these businesses, but we also want to draw in other potential customers from other parts of Tulsa.

When people do not look like you invest in your community, it may make you nervous. There have already been some rumblings like that over changes being made on the Historic Black Wall Street on Greenwood, a traditionally black marketplace. Hundreds of businesses were burned to the ground in 1921. Scores of people are used to mom-and-pop shops being in those locations, but those mom-and-pop shops are closed because rent is increased or business is not profitable. And some people get nervous about what is going to come into those locations.

Those locations may not be rented by black-owned businesses in the future, and it makes some people nervous. It also saddens some people and angers others. But the fact is, not all black people want to be entrepreneurs, and not all black-owned businesses are viable for brick-and-mortar locations. On the other hand, those who are thinking of coming into North Tulsa just to take money out of the area and not reinvest should expect to be closed for business sooner than later.

It is not difficult for businesses to come in, sell a great product or service, and donate a percentage of its profits to a local school in North Tulsa. It's not difficult for a business or organization to come into North Tulsa to partner with another organization there and host fundraisers that will help children, the elderly, or disabled people in the community. That's key to the success of the North Tulsa Renaissance. Reinvestment into the community by businesses in the community is necessary and should be expected. Not only do we want to see proposals for building new developments, but we also want to see the impact on North Tulsa.

The fear is real, and that fear can keep people from patronizing a business. As we all know, we generally spread bad news or bad service faster than we spread good news or good service. A new development was proposed a few years ago called Morton's Reserve. A development group purchased the property where the old Moton Hospital was built. The chairman is an African-American man who wants to revitalize that area. He wanted to build, develop, and create, which would have been a huge start for the North Tulsa Renaissance. The project has not moved forward as originally proposed but there seems to be a new plan with a partnership between the local development funder and the developer. They have amazing plans for the space which will be huge for North Tulsa. I hope the community supports the plans as this project can bring so much joy and love from to community.

Rather than the building sitting dormant for the next 50 years, there's going to be development for the first time in years. I am 41 years old, and I've never seen that building in use. So, we have someone who wants to develop the land and the property and create a beautiful workable space with retail. These partners are taking a major risk by investing in the community so I hope their investment provides generations of good jobs and economic development. I'm excited to see the people and groups who are trying to revitalize North Tulsa, and I'm all for it. I'm amazed at what they are planning to do, and I'm excited about the future of North Tulsa.

Hopefully, they'll have additional development plans to help North Tulsa to continue to realize its greatness. We may see pop-up shops, movie theaters, bars, walkable spaces, and retail spaces, which brings increases in sales tax revenue that will then go back into the community's schools. Not only does the community need retail and residental developments to succeed, but also our children's schools need these developments and future development to succeed. I look forward to the future the North Tulsa Renaissance.

The North Tulsa Renaissance

Chapter 14

The Great Depression Entrepreneur

During the time of the Tulsa Race Riots in 1921, the North Tulsa community was booming. Its people were able to provide for themselves as a community. They were entrepreneurs. Coming out of the difficulties of slavery and difficulties of racism and segregation came entrepreneurship. Entrepreneurship evolved out of necessity for the citizens of North Tulsa. They were segregated, and they were not allowed to rely on the government to subsidize farms and give them land the way others could. So, if they wanted something, they had to create it, build it, and support it. That is the framework for the North Tulsa Renaissance. We have to create, build, and support the new developments that will happen in North Tulsa.

A true entrepreneur sees a problem and finds a solution with technology, service, or products. It's vital for the realization of the North Tulsa Renaissance that entrepreneurs continue to do that. We must also accept that at some point, the entrepreneurs may not come from the North Tulsa community. But that doesn't mean we cannot support those developments. The goal is that North Tulsa starts to get the same resources, entertainment, and job opportunities as people on the other sides of the town. It will take years, but we have to have plans mapped out for that to happen.

The community can't rely on politicians or church leaders to solve all the problems. The community as a whole – including those politicians and church leaders – must work together to come up with the plan to realize North Tulsa's Renaissance. Once again, the community must create, build, and support. This framework will work. So many small areas in this country have banned together to improve their communities. The influx comes when investors and city leaders believe the community has a viable plan for improvement.

There are scores of entrepreneurs with the spirits of their Black Wall Street ancestors, and we must cultivate their talents and let them shine. Entrepreneurship is a prime factor of the North Tulsa Renaissance, whether it is through bakers, coders, builders, real estate investors, education innovation centers, or other elements. We must project ourselves not as victims but as crusaders, leaders, educators, risk-takers, planners, technology innovators, and survivors. Not even burning and killing our people should halt the greatness we were meant to create. Out of fire and ashes, out of death and destruction, out of hate and ignorance, rose children who would grow up to raise their own children to become doctors, lawyers, professors, police officers, entrepreneurs, and other professionals.

The North Tulsa Renaissance

Entrepreneurs today, as they did in 1921, deal with inherent challenges such as funding, planning, knowledge of market studies, and others. But the entrepreneurs on Black Wall Street were willing to take the risk to serve their people. They provided necessities that are still critical almost 100 years later. How have we allowed our community to go without the same resources it enjoyed almost a century ago? What do those early entrepreneurs think about how we have left the community? Would they be proud or disappointed? These questions should govern our efforts to improve the community.

North Tulsa is not a local phenomenon. It is nationally and even internationally known and recognized. Countries across oceans do not talk about South Tulsa or Downtown Tulsa or know the history like they know that of North Tulsa. The community has an opportunity to control the narrative, but we must be willing to step up and do our part. The great developments that will happen in North Tulsa will be celebrated internationally. We must have to show them who we are and what we are able to do for our community.

The entrepreneurs from the Great Depression dealt with greater injustices than we do today, which I am sure they hoped the future generations would not deal with: high levels of hate, discrimination, and bigotry. Unfortunately, 100 years later, the community still faces similar issues. It may not be at the level that it was 100 years ago, but it is still active in the Tulsa community. But those challenges are not non-starters. They are building blocks from which we can take the community over the top of ashes, death, and despair.

The North Tulsa Renaissance

We must not accept the status quo; we must not allow the victimization that was dealt us to allow us to give up the fight. For equal access to the American dream, we must not complain that opportunities are not available to our community. Real estate signs are up all over the area, ready to be taken down after the purchase of the property. We must not merely talk about buying the block but actually do it. It sounds good to say you are doing something for the community, but until you are invested in the community, you are just providing words. I wanted to do more than just talk about my ties to North Tulsa; I wanted to create my own legacy by investing in the community my grandmother once called home.

I hear so many times that Hispanic communities simply work together. They build, and then they support what's being built. They have entrepreneurs with food trucks, restaurants, grocery stores, retail outlets, car washes, and more. That segment of the community supports one another. This can also be said for white communities and the Asian communities that are also in North Tulsa. It is not said as much in the black community, and that's very unfortunate. I know black people do create, build, and support, but if we allow the stigma that black people don't support black people to seep into our brains, we will always believe that way.

African-Americans must do a better job of helping one another. African-Americans must do a better job of creating their own financial wealth and giving back. We must think bigger when it comes to any project or idea. If this were 1921 and the community did not have a grocery store, a group of people would band together and create a store with fewer resources, less government involvement, less education, less global knowledge, and less financial backing.

I am proud to see that we now have a group of investors planning to build a grocery store in the community. We must continue to support efforts to invest in North Tulsa, hold those investors accountable, and advocate for more investments. We must not stop with one grocery store, but we can use that project as a blueprint for additional development in North Tulsa.

Black Wall Street becomes a great buzzword for entrepreneurs because they want to invoke the spirit of the innovative entrepreneurs who once created Black Wall Street. The entrepreneurs during that era had the mindset that they had to create in order to save their families. They knew no one else was going to do it.

What always struck me was seeing pictures from the early 1900s and noticing how people dressed. The people, although cut off from the community south of the train tracks, dressed as professionally as they could. The less fortunate still dressed their children in a shirt and tie to go to school. They did not let their financial status to dictate their worth. We must teach our children that the way they carry themselves, whether they are poor or rich, truly matters. We must let our parents know that their sacrifices to dress their children in respectable clothing do not go unnoticed. Our future entrepreneurs are in North Tulsa, and we must groom them as such. We must teach them that even though their net monetary value may be negative, their personal value is worth more than gold.

The North Tulsa Renaissance

To create the next entrepreneurs, we must stress education – not just school education, but areas that will help our young people become the best versions of themselves, such as internet marketing, coding, financial literacy, tax laws, licensing, and trademarking. We must also focus on international business, contracting, real estate, technology, and innovation. There are future millionaires sitting in the classes of schools in North Tulsa, but we have not tapped into their millionaire mindset. Unlocking potential entrepreneur millionaires inside of our young people should be the main focus of leaders in the community. Don't just teach them how to fish: Teach them how to buy the land the pond is on, grow on the land, build on the land, lease their land, and sell the fish they catch.

The way to fight poverty is to promote education and entrepreneurship. Both areas of focus celebrate individualism, creativity, and ownership of knowledge, skills, and abilities. Young people have billions of dollars worth of resources in their hands daily. We must show them how to cultivate the knowledge provided to them for free and turn that knowledge into multiple streams of income. If a child is in a household with no or maybe one stream of income, how do we reach that child? We show him a better way to break the cycle of poverty, and that is through knowledge and effort. We should teach our children that school is their business and grades are their customer reviews.

When I was in high school, I wore a shirt and tie at least once or twice a week because I knew I wanted to be a businessperson. Even if our children do not want to be businessmen or women, there will be some form of business in their professions, so they should embrace it as soon as possible.

There are great entrepreneur mentors in the North Tulsa community. There are dentists, doctors, restaurant owners, nonprofit organization creators, and innovators. It is imperative that we link our students with these amazing people and their dynamic businesses and organizations. Internships are the real-world education many of our students need. These contacts could become lifelong mentors. This relationship is beneficial to both the mentor and the mentee, as the mentee could teach the mentor just as much as the mentor teaches the mentee.

Black people were the farmers of this country during slavery, but we have not passed on that knowledge to our children. Slavery left such a bad memory for generations that many people might not have wanted to relive the torture of long days of work with no pay. They may have thought they wanted to keep their children and grandchildren as far away from a plantation type of job as possible. Black people created millionaires during slavery, but the product that was sold for millions was not transferred to generations of black heirs. We think about the crops being the product that created millions, but it was actually the sale of black Africans who created the wealth. Black people have been entrepreneurs our entire existence, and we must continue to teach our children and communities how to keep the tradition going.

During the Great Depression in the early 1900s, members of the North Tulsa community knew they could not

The North Tulsa Renaissance

rely on their brothers and sisters in South Tulsa for help. Even after the destruction caused by hate, envy, and lack of knowledge, and one of the most notable domestic terrorism cases in history, North Tulsa rose above the hate and tried to rebuild. Their brothers and sisters from south of the railroad tracks did not help them rebuild, invest in reopening the businesses, or encourage their neighbors to do the right thing by breaking the barrier the railroad track created and shopping North. Per my research, I do know of members of South Tulsa trying to help some because many members of the North Tulsa community worked for people in South Tulsa.

We must not allow entrepreneurship to die. We must find ways to create small businesses that could one day become global businesses. And this has to have the support of the community. We have to channel the minds of the great entrepreneurs, physicians, builders, Masons, fraternity, and sorority members who built the community in the early 1900s and push forward the plan for development and support.

We must do everything we can to help those who want to become great entrepreneurs. With our collective resources, whether it is finances, accounting, marketing, or strategic planning, we can do it together. Our renaissance is now, and with a collective mindset of creating, build, and support, we will make our Black Wall Street ancestors proud. White communities built and learned from John D. Rockefeller and Andrew Carnegie their visions, and we must do the same with the vision of John B. Stradford and Dr. John Hope Franklin.

130

Successful communities learn from those who came before them. The Great Depression taught us a lot, and like the white entrepreneurs helped mold this country, the black entrepreneurs stood strong and created wealth for a community. Let's continue their legacy of black and white entrepreneurs on Black Wall Street. Let's globalize North Tulsa by showing the world that we are here to stay, build, create, and support.

The North Tulsa Renaissance

Chapter 15

Destination: North Tulsa

How do you sell North Tulsa? What values do the representatives of North Tulsa offer? If leaders in North Tulsa had to present the area to a panel of investors, what does that presentation look like? How do you speak of North Tulsa when you are engaging in conversations with your co-workers in South Tulsa? My opinion is that North Tulsa has an image problem compared with other parts of town. For years, we have allowed outsiders to control the narrative about North Tulsa. A person who cannot objectively take time to learn the history, engage with the community members, or see the needs of the community is not the person you want controlling your narrative.

If a candidate cannot articulate the value of North Tulsa or explain the benefits, needs, and opportunities to a panel of investors, the community should not elect him or her. We must move away from feel-good politics and shift to action-packed politics. All officials should be on the same page when it comes to North Tulsa. There should be a unified plan for all sectors. Areas that thrive in this country are destination communities. How do we make North Tulsa a place for out-of-state or even in-state travel? Can North Tulsa be a "staycation" destination? I believe it can.

Why are there no hotels in North Tulsa? Why are the main attractions a monument to death and destruction at the hands of racists, the Tulsa Zoo, and the Air and Space Museum? None of these would entice a business to bring 500 employees to the area to fill up a hotel. How do we change to an environment where business conferences are planned – if not to stay in North Tulsa, then to visit and spend money there? What does the City of Tulsa leadership say about North Tulsa? Do they ever pitch visiting the area to out-of-state people? "Destination North Tulsa" should be a top priority for city government. We see huge investments going into West Tulsa, but why not North Tulsa? How did North Tulsa fall down the priority list?

Some would say the focus of the community is wrong. What are the top three focal points for residents of North Tulsa? If the community cannot answer that, we have a challenge on our hands. A unified message is needed, but we can't have that with broken communication. The residents must know their diverse interests are going to be addressed. They must know they can not only want a focus on a grocery store in the area, but also other aspects such as police violence, mediocre education, lack of public funding and large-scale development projects, community beautification, etc. North Tulsa is not a one-topic community. It is diverse, educated, and eager for a better future for its children.

North Tulsa does not have to reinvent the wheel when it comes to improvements. We can mirror successful programs from other communities, other states, and even other countries. We must plant our feet on the ground and adopt a no-nonsense approach to change. The community must develop its own plans to rejuvenate the area. The beginning of the Black Wall Street was based on a plan to take care of the community. The beginning of the North Tulsa Renaissance will start with a similar plan.

To the doctors, lawyers, entrepreneurs, politicians, veterans, and community leaders who have preceded me, I pledge my undying respect for what you accomplished in the early 1900s. To those who were killed in the race massacre, I pledge my support for building the community back into something for which you can look down on us and smile about. Your blood and tears ran through the streets, and we now complain that someone else is not bringing development to the community. Your dreams of a vibrant North Tulsa will be recognized!

How do we get more people from South, East, and West Tulsa to visit North Tulsa? I think we must first desegregate our Sundays. Church members from all areas of town should visit the great churches in North Tulsa. A community church event is necessary. I would love to see those church members not only come to North Tulsa churches, but for members of churches in North Tulsa to go to other churches as well. A city that prays together stays together. We cannot showcase North Tulsa unless we showcase all aspects of North Tulsa. We must let other communities know that North Tulsa is not just open for interfaith and interdenominational worship but also open for business.

North Tulsa must become a hub for innovative entrepreneurship. The area must land large manufacturing contracts and become the most talked-about area in town. The eternal pessimist will say this is impossible. To them, I offer these precedents: Las Vegas was built in an area that has less development than North Tulsa. Harlem did not become the great area it is now by allowing other communities to dictate its worth. No one leader or group can create the North Tulsa Renaissance, but with the help of hundreds of people, the turnaround will happen. The planning of a few will lead to the implementation set forth by thousands of people.

North Tulsa needs highly skilled workers to fill jobs that will hopefully come to the area. The last thing we would want is for a factory to decide it wants to house a corporate location in North Tulsa but not be able to find any skilled labor from the area. We must ensure that our children are graduating and getting post-high school education. We must actively train community members on basic skills needed for employment, such as word-processing skills, telephone skills, critical thinking skills, project management, negotiation, resume building, medical terminology, and coding, etc. Community members must educate themselves on skills needed to find jobs less dependent on the government and more dependent on the needs of the community and international customers.

Riding through North Tulsa and then through South Tulsa tells the true tale of two cities. The South Tulsa Renaissance happened years ago with investment from government, local and international companies, increased high school graduation rates, workforce training programs, and a motivated community that wanted walkable spaces, great schools, less crime, more retail, more jobs, and a higher quality of life. What part of that is different from the wish list for any resident of North Tulsa? The answer is none. In the case of South Tulsa, people had to take risks for the sake of their community and potential profits. A renaissance or resurgence comes from risk and pride. North Tulsa has pride, and we just need people who are willing to take the risk for the greater good of the community and the potential for large profits.

The beautification of North Tulsa is essential if it is to become a destination area. Boarded-up houses only attract drugs, theft, and other crimes. Those houses do not instill a sense of pride in a community. How can we sell North Tulsa if hundreds of houses sit vacant and boarded up? Tulsa needs an ordinance that bans boarded-up homes. Such an ordinance was adopted in North Carolina in 2015. This ordinance made it a requirement to register a house an owner planned to board up. Owners of vacant or deteriorated houses have 30 days to register the property and pay a $500 fee every 90 days until the house meets guidelines. An additional $500 could be assessed to the owner if he or she fails to register every 90 days. This ordinance brings revenue to the city in the form of registration fees, and it offers a deterrent for owners who may continue allowing homes to deteriorate, thus bringing down the value of the area.

I would like to see a Tulsa ordinance go one step further. I agree with North Carolina's ordinance, but I would like stricter language incorporated into the Tulsa ordinance. There should be a requirement that within 90 days, the property must be without boards and either for sale or rent.

The North Tulsa Renaissance

If the owner does not comply, he or she gets an additional 30 days to comply, or the house will become the property of the City of Tulsa. The property would then be sold in an annual auction – hopefully to local investors who will take better care of the property. This ordinance can be a great money generator for the city. The portion of the revenue should be allocated to the area of town that generated the increased income. This regulation could help limit the number of derelict houses in the city. It will require vetting and improving, but it is a good start.

Is North Tulsa the dirty little secret the City of Tulsa does not want visitors to know about? Does the low voter participation in North Tulsa indicate this area does not want to be recognized as a powerful community in the city? Does the lack of investment from previous residents of North Tulsa mean those individuals do not care about the community and they have left it to rot? I do not believe so. I think the City of Tulsa understands that with a strong North, Tulsa comes to a strong Tulsa. I do not believe many people know exactly what it will take to advance the community past where it is right now. In Downtown and Southwest Tulsa, they know investment has been the key to the resurgence of those areas. Logic suggests this model could be replicated in North Tulsa, but it has not happened thus far. That is because North Tulsa has a public relations problem, both internally and externally. For years, North Tulsa has been playing on the junior varsity team, while Downtown and South Tulsa have been working to "go pro." A portion of that reasoning is due to stagnant leadership and a lack of innovative thinking.

The North Tulsa Renaissance

We need a VisionNorthTulsa2025 project that will allow the area to gain access to tax revenue, grant funding, and private and public funding. North Tulsa has a chance to be the shining light of the city, but people are apprehensive about investing because they feel they will be betting on a losing dream. I see both great opportunity and need in North Tulsa, but the challenge is getting others to see it as well.

A modern-day Reginald Lewis is needed for the community. He was the first African-American to be accepted into Harvard without a formal application. He graduated from Harvard Law and, after working for a law firm for two years, and then he started his own law firm. His passion was business takeovers, first increasing a company's value and then selling the company. His first venture was a $22 million deal that eventually netted him $50 million. He was a great philanthropist, giving to a number of charities.

We need an investment group, such as The North Tulsa Investment Group (NTIG), that is born out of the community and allows for public and private investment to purchase and develop the community. There are multimillion-dollar companies housed in North Tulsa, and with a vetted plan, I am sure they would entertain investing in an area that will help benefit their employees and provide a boost to their local and international brands. Raising capital is a difficult endeavor, and any investment group needs guidance and mentoring.

I would love to see investment groups gain assistance from established investment conglomerates to learn the business, review pros and cons, and establish a relationship that will help grow the NTIG. The investment group would operate on the main premise of growing North Tulsa's tax revenue, creating jobs, establishing innovative school initiatives, and owning as much land and property as possible. A branch of the group would be responsible for community outreach, working with local nonprofits, churches, public safety, and educational leaders to discuss the needs of the community. Bringing back retail should be a primary purpose of the investment group. The community needs coffee shops, restaurants, movie theaters, bowling alleys, kids' party places, grocery stores, bars, and comedy clubs. North Tulsa also needs medical organizations such as urgent care facilities, veterans' care clinics, and an acute care hospital.

Gaining access to capital is the key to success. Knowledge about operating the right business for the customers is another key. The NTIG would have varying levels of investment opportunities that would allow community members to participate in the change that is coming to North Tulsa. The group would have to manage a multimillion-dollar fund. Raising that kind of capital can be a challenge, but I see it as one that is vital to the success of a community. I see the challenge as lifesaving. Currently, North Tulsa residents are more likely to live fewer years than their brothers and sisters who live in other parts of Tulsa. The group must address that issue head-on and make improvements to that statistic.

Destination North Tulsa can be realized with the continued push from the community. Residents have been doing great things over the past five to 10 years, and with their continued work, North Tulsa will thrive. I want to thank all the people who serve on committees, lead organizations, provide safety to the community, operate a business in the area, invest in the housing market, and faith leaders who have provided spiritual guidance, as well as our veterans who were willing to give their lives to protect our communities. Without them, North Tulsa could not have the great community that it has. We have a lot of work to do, but what is work without a great outcome? Together, we are better!

The North Tulsa Renaissance

Chapter 16

The Wolves of Black Wall Street

The North Tulsa Renaissance cannot happen without understanding where we came from. Our current liberties were not just recognized; they were fought for, and it required death. Many black people fought in the U.S. Army during the Civil War and World Wars II, and I but when they came back to their country, they were not treated as war heroes. Before Oklahoma became a state, Tulsa was a booming area for black entrepreneurs, leaders, preachers, doctors, lawyers, and educators. Tulsa was segregated, as most of the country was at that time. As Oklahoma moved to statehood, the Democratic Party leaders made sure the first bill to be signed was to segregate the state. From its inception, Oklahoma was racist.

Starting a business is its own version of war. Of course, that's not to the extent of a bloody battle, but it's a war nonetheless. The leaders and entrepreneurs who decided to put their life's' savings on the line and start businesses on Greenwood in Tulsa, Oklahoma, were pioneers and heroes. Their sacrifice of time, money, blood, and reputation were forever immortalized when their businesses, lives, and dreams were taken from them during the race massacre of 1921.

To operate a business during times before the Great Depression was a legendary feat. In 1921, America was involved in World War I. Most of the community in North Tulsa moved there for better opportunities. Oklahoma was seen as safe and thriving territory for African-Americans. Many of the entrepreneurs in North Tulsa were one or two generations removed from slavery. It is important to look at this context: Africans were kidnapped from their homes and sold into slavery. They were placed on death ships with other Africans from different tribes, and many of them were not able to speak the languages of their captures or captives.

Movies often depict Africans speaking English. This is necessary, so English-speaking people can follow the storylines, but the reality was that the Africans spoke their native languages. Movies and books also depict African slaves as savages, monsters, less than human, uneducated, and easily manipulated. In Africa, men and women were kings, scholars, warriors, politicians, and leaders. How do you think you would fare if you were taken out of your homeland and taken to another land that was stolen and then forced to work for free?

If Africans were such savages, how did they become multilingual, pick up new techniques, learn to read, figure out how to use weapons foreign to them, and invent great products and machines that are still in use today? The future "Wolves of Black Wall Street" descended from these kings, leaders, and scholars. They took the pride, sense of community, hunger for a better life, and determination from their parents or grandparents, who may have been slaves.

Upon dirt and rocks, entrepreneurs built Black Wall Street. They realized they were not second-class citizens, and they created their own wealth. The entrepreneurs in North Tulsa were doing better than many of their white counterparts on the south side of the railroad tracks, and their success created animosity and jealousy. The wealth allowed members of the community to own cars, travel, and provide a prosperous living for their families.

Inside the mind of an entrepreneur is an insatiable eagerness to succeed. A sense of ownership is ingrained in America, and the wolves of Black Wall Street knew that. With the knowledge of the fact that God is not making any more land, the black landowners wanted to own as much as they could. North Tulsa was a gold rush for once-owned people. They wanted the American dream of ownership. Is this sense of ownership importance conveyed to our young people today? Is the sense of creating something that will feed the family inoculated into the community of North Tulsa? Is the importance of entrepreneurship taught in North Tulsa? The answers to these questions maybe yes, but the teachings are not widespread enough.

The first wolf of Black Wall Street was O.W. Gurley, a man who created the first grocery store in North Tulsa. The area had its first grocery store in the early 1900s, and after 100 years, there are now two grocery stores in North Tulsa as of 2019. That is the harsh reality of stagnant growth lagging far behind the other parts of the city south of the railroad track.

The North Tulsa Renaissance

According to research, Mr. Gurley wanted to become rich and politically powerful. He was born in 1988 to two former slaves. He became a landowner when most African-Americans did not own land. He not only built a grocery store, but he founded a rooming house as well, which is similar to a hotel or bed-and-breakfast. He is credited with naming the Greenwood district. He created what is now known as Vernon AME church. Mr. Gurley amassed over $200,000 worth of commercial property that included a billiard parlor, barbershop, pool hall, cigar shop, and more. But during the race massacre of 1921, he lost everything. His commercial buildings and personal residence were burned to the ground. He lost what is equivalent to $2.6 million in today's money. Though he was an amazing, influential pioneer, Mr. Gurley could not have known how his life could motivate so many.

Other wolves of Black Wall Street are:

- Dr. A. C. Jackson, a prominent surgeon who assisted patients of all races.

- John and Loula Williams, proprietors of The DreamLand Theaters, which had a capacity of 650 seats. This was a symbol of excellence in the community. Mrs. Williams was known as one of the most proficient businesswomen.

- J. B. Stradford, one of the richest African-Americans in Tulsa. He made his money by being a rental property owner, initiating the development of Greenwood, and he owned the largest African-American hotel in the United States. He and 19 other

African-American men were indicted for starting a riot during the race massacre. It wasn't until 1996 that the charges were dropped.

- A.J. Smitherson, a scholar who wielded great political power. He started the Daily Tulsa Star, a newspaper from 1913 until his office building was burned down in the race massacre of 1921. During the time of racial unrest, he worked with statewide government to bring to justice the perpetrators who burned 30 homes in Dewey, Oklahoma.

- Simon Berry, who eventually became the largest employer of black people. He was a pioneer in the transportation industry, adding chartered planes and buses to his fleet.

- James Goodwin, who was considered by many as the "founding father" of Black Wall Street. As a young man, he worked as a store clerk, but after some time, he became the youngest entrepreneur in Greenwood history. He started the Oklahoma Eagle, which continues operations to this day.

There are many entrepreneurs who take up the torch and are investing their money, time, and effort into seeing the dreams of our early entrepreneurs realized. Black Wall Street is not what it used to be, but it is still around, more than 100 years later. Not many institutions can say that. The proud and brilliant entrepreneurs who walked the streets of North Tulsa are remembered for paving the way for the entrepreneurial spirit that is alive on Black Wall Street now. It takes a lot of pride and openness to risk opening a business in a building that is older than most around it, but the Black Wall Street entrepreneurs are up to any challenge.

I have had the pleasure of visiting or patronizing a few businesses currently housed in the Black Wall Street buildings, and I have been impressed at what is happening in the area. Art, food, social work services, and entertainment are all in evidence on Black Wall Street. It is not what it once was, but it is very impressive to see old buildings revitalized. Long are gone the movie theaters, pharmacies, hotels, and other original businesses from the Greenwood blocks, but the spirit of the early entrepreneurs and supporters still lives on in today's entrepreneurs.

The future of Black Wall Street will depend on how the young wolf pups are raised to understand entrepreneurship. They should be exposed to the story of the Wolves of Black Wall Street as much as possible to see history repeat itself. The young wolves will be the ones to innovate Black Wall Street into the next generation. Our youth need to learn and respect the history-changing events that lead to the destruction of our people and their lifelong dreams.

There is a current power struggle for Black Wall Street. Outside investors are trying to purchase the buildings and land, and organizations are starting with the Black Wall Street moniker to advocate for the area, and there is confusion about the role or goal of Black Wall Street is right now. There is no unified voice for the current Black Wall Street, but there are bright spots, such as the new art gallery on Greenwood, whose owner brings together black and white artists to showcase their works to the community. There are more white faces and brown faces on Greenwood than in previous years, which is amazing. This blueprint needs to be reproduced throughout North Tulsa. Money is green, support is green, and love is free, so we should welcome it into not only Black Wall Street but to the other potential Black Wall Street-type areas where development, culture, love, and support are visible.

I have no doubt in my mind that the initial entrepreneurs on Black Wall Street envisioned a Black Wall Street throughout North Tulsa. If these plans had come to pass, North Tulsa would have been in stiff competition with other areas of the city for development bids, relocating business headquarters, and investments. Hundreds of millionaires would have been created, colleges would have been founded, hospitals would have been erected, and the school system would have been one of the top ones in the state. The amount of land owned by the initial Black Wall Street entrepreneurs would have made way for future developments. They owned, they created, they built, and they innovated.

What should become of Black Wall Street now? Expansion is the only option for a successful Black Wall Street. There are currently three areas primed and ready for Black Wall Street expansion: 36th and Peoria, Pine and Peoria, and Apache and Martin Luther King Jr. are areas that substantial investment could allow the area to flourish. I would never want to take away from the true history of Black Wall Street, but we can no longer look at the Greenwood areas as a stopping point. O.W. Gurley would have loved to see his vision of an economically booming North Tulsa realized. As we work to solidify and prop up the historic Black Wall Street, we should be working with city government and the private sector to expand Tulsa's continuing growth to identified areas in North Tulsa ready for development.

I can only hope to accomplish even half of what the early entrepreneurs of North Tulsa were able to achieve. Within their lifetimes, they created something that has been discussed for almost 100 years. That contribution to historical significance is right up there with the Industrial Revolution, the technology bubble, and other monumental moments in our country's history.

Walking the streets of Black Wall Street, I feel a sense of ownership of the current North Tulsa community's lack of development. I feel a sense of shame that I have not done enough to make my grandmother proud of what I have built, developed, and created. That shame, doubt, and eagerness to make ancestors proud are what drives many entrepreneurs to be successful.

What will be your role in the North Tulsa Renaissance? Will you be a creator, a builder, a supporter, an entrepreneur, a community organizer, a politician, an investor, a leader, an educator, an innovator, or all of the above? We all have roles to play in the resurgence of North Tulsa. We must take up those roles, research them, and lead with them. We must be the change that we want to see.

If you want to be part of this movement, learn the inside of government and how you can use partnerships to decrease costs and increase profits. Create nonprofit organizations to oversee your for-profit ventures. Purchase land and real estate and change the landscape of North Tulsa for the better. Stay strong, because the naysayers will attack you. They attacked community changers in 1920, and they created history. Don't conform to what has not worked for 100 years. Create your own lane and allow others to follow. Step out on faith with a vetted plan. Go over your numbers twice. Never trust anyone 100 percent. Get a non-disclosure to protect your idea but seek guidance from industry experts, potential customers, and others who will not benefit from your success or failure.

The renaissance is happening and will continue. The chapters have been being written for years, and thanks to the steadfast support from the community, the entrepreneurs, politicians, and leaders have benefited. Let's keep the Wolves of Black Wall Street in our prayers, thoughts, and good vibes. But also, we must send them customers, referrals, and suggestions.

In this day and age, it is harder for a company to survive and thrive with only black support, even though the black dollar accounts for $1.5 trillion of spending power, and if that amount were a country, it would be the 15th largest country in the world. We must turn the black dollar into the global dollar, kick open the doors and make our dollar count. We must attract dollars from all people to sustain, give back to the community, and grow. This is not the case for every industry, but some need diverse dollars to succeed.

The Wolves of Black Wall Street should be celebrated for their courage to take up the mantle and create, build, and develop. As more entrepreneurs jump into the arena, the community will continue to flourish. I am encouraged and

The North Tulsa Renaissance

motivated by their sacrifice, and I hope others will follow in
their footsteps.

Chapter 17

The Change Agents

From kings, to hanging fruit, to a revolution, to the present day, we hold the keys to the North Tulsa Renaissance. The youth are the key to a successful community. The knowledge they possess can change thinking, circumstances, and generations. The power within young minds is limitless.

How do we tap into that power? We engage. We must engage with our youth in the community. They will become the wealth generators of the future, but I feel they are overlooked because they are young. Many do not view them as a politically important group because they are young. They have the opportunity to drastically change the political, global, and economic landscape of the world. It is the job of the adults to cultivate the knowledge, energy, innovative thoughts, and networks to help our youth realize their true potential.

When you are a child, your parents tell you that you can be anything you want to be when you grow up. Where does that belief go when a child becomes a young adult? If we are not advising our youth to reach for their lofty dreams, we are doing both them and our country a disservice. The youth of every generation have wanted to forge their own paths. Many have chafed at the notion that they had to follow their mothers' or fathers' dreams. They wanted their own dreams, and many of them fought and died for those dreams.

New entrepreneurs, doctors, educators, politicians, and public safety leaders may today be impoverished. Our next great inventor may be living in a low-income house with a lack of community motivation, home support, and adult vision. Reaching that young person is fundamental to the North Tulsa Renaissance. Every movement needs energy, youth, and ideas, and our current youth are the key to the moment. They must recognize that themselves and fight for their piece of history. Will they pave the way or be paved over? Will they be agents of change, or will they allow change to happen without their input? I believe the youth of today will rise up and take their proper position as a game-changer when it comes to technology, racial understanding, global coordination, creating a level playing field, and needed reforms such as prison, voting, and rights of others.

During the civil rights movement, young people created a culture of love, coordination, faith, peace, and an appetite for change. The young people saw a country that did not identify with their wants and needs, and they worked hard to create a better country. The present-day youth may also see a country that has left them to flap in the wind. The adults who are supposed to look out for the youth have stood by while local governments voted to decrease funding for child health care and education. Without proper education, that future leader who may be impecunious could possibly never realize his or her greatness.

The leaders of the early 19th century took it upon themselves to educate themselves because they knew others were not looking out for their best interests. They created their own community. The youth of today can create their own virtual communities and push for change. They can communicate through chat rooms, Google hangouts, Instagram Live, and other social media. No community revitalization should be implemented without consulting the youth of America because when many of the current adults are retiring, the youth of today will come into power. When enhancing a community, we must think of the projects as businesspeople would. For a business to survive, it must look to its customers to see what they are willing to support, and the young people in the community are the customers of the community who will one day become the owners of the community.

When adults are fighting over which stores to allow into their community instead of fighting for sustainable opportunities for the youth, there is a real disconnect. A small box store will possibly create five jobs, but it also creates tax revenue for the community. A focused fight to keep those stores out of the North Tulsa Renaissance is shortsighted. I would rather see a fight for bringing jobs to the community, for all high schools in North Tulsa to have an 80 percent graduation rate, for partnering with local and national companies to provide internships and scholarships to high school students. I would also like to see a coordinated community effort to reach out to the impoverished, who have a likelihood of being imprisoned if they do not graduate high school and attend a college program.

Our young people have to sit and think the adults are not fighting for them because the agendas of many continue to oppress them. If you are a young person and you have grown up in a community where there are hundreds of boarded-up houses, but many adults are not focused on improving that, you may feel they do not want to truly improve the area. If you are a young person and you do not have an innovative community center that will allow you to hone your skills, meet like-minded people, create substantive solutions, and effect change, you may think your community has nothing to offer you.

The North Tulsa Renaissance is partially dependent on young people who have graduated from college or trade school and want to come back to North Tulsa to live while they start their professional careers. We need their newly gained knowledge of world events, leaders, business principles, and elevated thought processes. We need the youth to come back and invest in their communities. Hundreds of thousands of dollars of investment go across the state border every day that could have been used to build up North Tulsa or communities like it. Just as the U.S. government is trying to repatriate billions of dollars from offshore banks, North Tulsa must repatriate thousands and possibly millions of dollars that have left the community. Imagine if people from the North Tulsa community who have moved away started coming back to invest in North Tulsa real estate. There would no better landlord investor than someone who loves his or her community or someone who has a tie to the community.

In America, we are the land of the imprisoned, and unfortunately, many of our youth are behind prison bars instead of running their own bars. If young people and adults are to be agents of change, they have to educate themselves, listen to one another, and work toward a community that sees retail, grocery stores, and influence becomes a reality. The change that we all want to see is clear, but we cannot get past our own agendas. Everyone wants power, but few are exhibiting the power to create businesses and lead a community.

If we are going to bring a North Tulsa Renaissance to fruition, we have to start thinking like the other areas of the city that are booming. In North Tulsa, there is a sense of a need to get the entire community behind an idea for it to work, but that is not how business works. You must have customers to maintain a viable business, but if you cannot get the entire community's head around an idea, you have to think about how many people you will actually need to make your business or organization successful. It is important to remember that just because you start a business in the community doesn't mean your only customers and supporters should come from that community. You must be able to expand your influence beyond a certain zip code.

There are deep-rooted feelings about North Tulsa. So many want to see improvement, but the agents of change must multiply and influence all areas of North Tulsa. The young people must be the agents of change so they can influence their peers and encourage them not only to excel and graduate from high school but also to volunteer in the community, go to college and help the community in some capacity upon graduation. The adults in the community must focus not just on social change, which is important, but also on financial dominance. The North Tulsa community in 1921 was rebuilt with no loans, no insurance settlements, and with the spirit of change and perseverance. If they can do that, today's community can band together and generate more wealth than this area has ever seen.

Even if pro-North Tulsa officials are elected, that does not guarantee prosperity or that we will see new businesses moving into the community, generating jobs and tax dollars. Our officials must agree to be held to a high standard. For the community to succeed, the education depression must be addressed. Schools must no longer be allowed to be pipelines for private prisons, low-paying jobs, and low-skilled workers. We must find a way to change the mindset on what it means to have pride in North Tulsa. The loudest person must no longer control the agenda, but the entire community must control it.

We must cultivate immense pride and unity in North Tulsa and work on five main areas of importance. We must track both the accomplishments and failures, along with the performance of our elected officials, leaders of schools, and local organizations. North Tulsa should have its own form of a Better Business Bureau for certain areas of interest, such as political, educational, and business. All politicians should have websites that show their active and previous projects, yearly accomplishments, agenda and promises, and their challenges.

The North Tulsa Renaissance

It is important for the community to see all the great things our elected officials accomplish and to ensure they are meeting their constituents' needs. Principals of our schools and business leaders would also be listed. It is imperative to hold them to the task of working to better implement real change in the community. The principals would be tracked and graded on how they treat their teachers, how the grades and test scores improve or decline, and their schools' graduation rates. Businesses would be graded for customer interactions, professionalism, and contributions to the community. When an individual's performance is tracked, the performance generally gets even better. It would be beneficial to have an organization or company help build and maintain these sites. That company could also help track and report the calls, emails, and letters that come in about the politicians, educators, or businesses in North Tulsa. This is not meant to be a gossip forum or an avenue for haters to thrive, but rather a tool to make our community better.

Change starts with people not wanting to go back where they were previously, but unfortunately, many in North Tulsa would have had more retail, grocery options, and family-friendly businesses almost 100 years ago than today. That harsh reality is why the North Tulsa Renaissance is so important. We must bring the community back to an even level than it enjoyed in 1921 when it comes to economic development. We always have young people who want to leave the community because they cannot identify with the culture, the lack of resources to help them to thrive, or the failure to change negative perceptions in place since they were babies. They do not feel safe, they are tired of being surrounded by boarded-up houses, and they do not see employment opportunities. We have to change that because the young people in our community make our community.

Many programs are already providing exceptional education to our students in North Tulsa, but some are lagging behind. Schools can do a great job in pre-kindergarten and elementary education, but if the high schools in a community are substandard, the students will suffer, which means the community suffers. There's nothing wrong with looking at best practices from other schools in the city, or even in other cities, to see how those practices can be implemented into North Tulsa schools. There are schools that can boast a 100 percent graduation rate. Granted, those schools are generally smaller than the schools in North Tulsa, but maybe some of the principles can be applied here. Local charter schools are doing great things for students, and we should build on that.

I have seen a considerable amount of passion generated for certain topics, so I know there is a base of support in the community. We must harness the passion and allow it to improve and grow our community. An engaged community is healthy, vibrant, resilient, and prosperous. The North Tulsa delegation must-attend local city meetings, country proposals, education service center meetings, panel discussions concerning others areas of the city, and other gatherings that will improve community-based knowledge. The more we know, the better we know.

Chapter 18

The Perpetual Slave Ship

We have all heard about the horrors of the Transpacific Slave Trade, wherein men and women were tied up like animals in unthinkable conditions. We have all heard of desperate men and women who decided to take their own lives rather than be subjected to the oppression, rape, and violence that awaited them in America. The slave ship is a symbol of stolen riches. The men and women were rich resources in their villages. They were the leaders, educators, medicine people, and breadwinners for their families. But people who looked like them and were then sold again into slavery by people who did not look like them sold them into slavery. They were placed on slave ships with others who did not speak their language, but they shared one thing: Their voyage would forever change their lives.

The thieves of African riches thought, less of the people who would become purchased property. They knew that for them to have a rich lineage themselves, they had to steal and kill. Their lack of meaningful education prompted them to leave their families with the shame and stigma of promoting slavery, rather than seek other opportunities to leave their future family with stories of how they built businesses from the ground up and raised generations with dignity. Rather than their descendants being able to state they are proud of their white heritage, they have made it unpopular to do so. Their selfish actions forever tainted their blood and names.

The harbingers of death left their families to try hard to wipe away the stench of blood, sweat, and tears of stolen people. The generations of young people do not know what their ancestors did and caused during the early history of this country. The perpetuation of evil using the words of our biblical father to enslave, punish, and rape was the norm during the days of slavery. The captives who would eventually become bilingual would also learn to read a foreign language and teach hundreds of capturers what culture meant, although we were viewed in the same way as cattle. Our ancestors were considered property that could be willed from one generation to the next.

Slavery became a mindset for many who saw the generational oppression of their people. It became the norm to be raised and die in slavery. The so-called masters, who actually mastered nothing, would force captives to believe in their god and the scriptures they read and enfolded the way of life called "slavery." The truth is, Christianity would have moved through all continents as it has without the brutality used to expand it. The way they keep slavery active for 400 years was to keep their captured people dumb, beaten down, dependent, and hopeless. Unfortunately, the capturers and slave owners did not know the slaves were not dumb. They were able to withstand punishment, and they hoped that God would provide salvation for them.

Wood and water were the vessels for slavery in America. The ocean will forever be the resting place for many of our ancestors. Slavery also changed the landscape of family ties. Before slavery, the only link between our white brothers and sisters was that we all came from the same continent. During the rape culture perpetuated during slavery, we became closer blood brothers and sisters and rightful owners of millions of acres of land in America.

We have now allowed ourselves to kill one another over land that should have been ours, but that we now rent. I say this with the knowledge of the true landowners on this continent, the Native Americans. Lying, stealing, raping, and murdering were taught to generations of people as they saw a better way forward to steal land from the rightful owners. Why wouldn't slavery be another feather in their hats?

Many people think marijuana is a gateway drug but stealing, lying, raping, and murder form a gateway to more stealing, lying, raping, and murdering for generations. To own land was one of the proudest moments of our ancestors' lives, but we are now content with paying other men's mortgages and demolishing our own communities. Our former slave owners would be proud of the culture they created. They generated the hate we have for one another. They created the crab-in-the-barrel mentality we have, along with the desecration of our women that we now perpetuate.

Why do we continue to allow the slave owners to win? When will we turn the tide and raise the dreams of our dead ancestors, who fought and died, and were raped, beaten, mutilated, and humiliated, just so we could take them for granted? How sad that our community has not forged ahead in the same way as leaders, educators, entrepreneurs, scholars, kings and queens, innovators, and medical innovators who would have become something greater than slaves if given a chance.

We must not allow our current generation's physical bodies to be the new slave ships, with their minds being the water that brings them to the destruction of their people. Our youth are the new rich resources that are planted in this country. Will they grow this country or destroy it? The previous generations had the chance to lead our youth, and the opportunity to lay the framework for a prosperous future. The slave ships brought us over to this soil, but the new "yachts" are our destiny. We must not allow our community to be the new "strange fruit," sacrificed on the "poplar trees." We must teach our community members that they can own the same land where their ancestors were lynched, beaten, raped, and murdered.

When you hear racist people talk about "taking the country back" for which they stole, murdered, and raped, it is incredible that they have not realized that their ancestors were unwanted guests. Slaves were stolen from one of the richest continents known to man and brought to a continent that these slaves turned into another rich continent. We must never allow others to tell us that we do not belong here because it is very likely that they truly do not belong here themselves.

The key to realizing the dreams of a people is creating a wealth channel for the community. When other cultures are leaving hundreds of thousands of dollars to the next generation through life insurance, homeownership, stocks/mutal funds, and other investments, we must make sure we are not merely leaving GoFundMe log-ins, six-month leases, and unprofitable debt. We can change a generation by investing in ourselves, so we will leave our lineage with wealth.

Adults can start a custodial investment account for their younger children which will allow the child to have a growing investment that can last a lifetime. As the stock market goes up, the child will reap the gains in the future. Even if you are living paycheck to paycheck, if you can invest $20-$30 per month over the next 15-20 years, your child may not fall victim to generational poverty. Fidelity is a great company to start your child's investment accout. We can create our own generational wealth with a small amount of investment into ourselves.

The North Tulsa Renaissance

Chapter 19

The North Tulsa Repatriation Act

N orth Tulsa has produced some of the greatest people ever known. It has created, supported, and advocated for some of the most successful people to come out of the state of Oklahoma. North Tulsa is a hub of love, excitement, and passion. But what happens when the resources you create to be stellar employees, NFL football stars, educators, politicians, businessmen, and women are then not able to repatriate their funds back into the community?

Some people who grew up in North Tulsa can't wait to move out of the area and never return. Some get upset at the fact that people left North Tulsa and moved farther south or out of the state. They really don't move back into the community. So, let's look at how that affects the entire area when the community has supported an individual who has gone off to become successful, received an education, started her own business, secured a good job, is doing well for herself, but the dollars she earns may not make it back to North Tulsa.

The North Tulsa Renaissance

The repatriation of dollars is fundamental to the North Tulsa Renaissance. We need those young professionals who have obtained their education and succeeded to spend their dollars back with North Tulsa businesses. The community's job is to give those people an avenue or a venue in which to put their dollars. I know several people who have come out of North Tulsa, but they just haven't seen an avenue for repatriating money back into the community. I believe we have a unique opportunity to bring millions of dollars back into the community from people who were born here or who have ties here but may have left for one reason or the other. So, picture someone who obtained a master's degree and is now a successful lawyer living in Colorado or Chicago or Florida but grew up in North Tulsa. Imagine what would happen if we could reach that person and give him an avenue to invest in North Tulsa and help the community bring about revitalization. It boosts the community that helps people who grew up there to see how their dollars can really have an effect on the lives of people who remain behind.

It's essential that investment or development groups be created for North Tulsa, but if there were opportunities established and promoted for people who live outside the community – or even people who live in the community and want to see great things happening in North Tulsa – that would be the ideal scenario. Many would love to see their investment dollars go into the building, creating and cultivating change in North Tulsa.

Many families have seen their community members grow up in the same houses from generation to generation. They have attended the same schools and walked the same streets, and they have similar dreams for the community. Those same people have seen scores of others leave North Tulsa, never to return.

The history that is not pushed forward to the younger generation is staggering. The stories from grandma are not as vivid and intact because the elder matriarch is now 40 instead of 68. We don't sit around the dinner tables as we used to and enjoy grandma's cooking because the grandmothers of today are much younger and extremely vested in trying to keep food on the table for their children and grandchildren. The history shared by 65- and 75-year-old Americans is our greatest lost treasure if it is not listened to or sought after.

My grandmother tried to teach me how to make her signature jelly recipe when I was a teenager, but like many young adults of today, I was too busy to learn something from her. She instead took her potentially million-dollar recipe with her to the grave. This happens daily around the world. The missed millions, which are the million-dollar ideas, are buried in the soil of America.

College and trade schools are the foundation for powering the North Tulsa Renaissance because with education comes opportunity, changed paradigms, and advancing ideals needed for success. When a young adult goes away to college, he knows his mom is still living in the apartments or in the house in North Tulsa, and he knows that for him to truly help his community, he must be the one to make it. Not only do we need these young adults to make something of themselves, but we also need them to do their part to make our communities even better, more efficient, innovative, and more collaborative. Once the students become graduates, they can start working or creating their own companies and bring to fruition the success they've dreamed of for years. With their uplifting experiences, struggles, and networking, they will be able to pass on their knowledge not only to the community but also to their own families. They will be able to encourage the younger population, and even the older ones, to strive to unlock the greatness inside of themselves.

The greatest tragedy in North Tulsa is that the community does not retain its talent and leaders because there is no sustainable mechanism to entice them to stay, invest, and create here. This is true for hundreds of communities around the country. How do we keep our young leaders and entice those who have left the community to return to lend their input and talents to realizing the dreams of the entrepreneurs and leaders who built Black Wall Street?

We also leave our most vulnerable, impressionable, and talented young people in substandard situations. We cannot control the households in which they live, but we have an opportunity to help mold young leaders, scientists, and entrepreneurs by reaching them before, during, and after school. We must create summer programs that prepare our children for the future and not just allow them to settle for their substandard reality. Our greatest investment in North Tulsa should be the investment in our children and young adults because they have the best opportunity of any generation to repatriate back to North Tulsa once they have gained a higher level of learning and thinking.

Investors don't like to throw money at bad ideas. Many people may feel North Tulsa is a bad investment, but I disagree. As someone who has at this moment invested almost $450,000 in real estate in North Tulsa, I see the long-term opportunities. There is a low barrier to entry and plenty of inventory and willing rental property seekers. While continuing to promote homeownership, it is important for an investor to provide a service for the residents in any community. The individuals in North Tulsa need quality shelter, and my goal is to provide that to as many people as possible. Other investors have that opportunity as well. Instead of seeing North Tulsa as a boarded-up community, we must view it as a gift waiting to be opened and appreciated.

I've seen the excitement and the pride of the community during sporting events and Juneteenth celebrations. We must build on that excitement and keep it going throughout the year. We must celebrate the phenomenal things our young people do and help provide them what they need to be successful. The same groups of hundreds of people who celebrate during pivotal moments throughout the year have the ability to create significant financial opportunities in North Tulsa. But where do they put their money? After buying a meal at a food truck, where do they put their money? After buying a T-shirt, where does that money go? Where are the wealth-generating opportunities for these individuals, who may or may not live in North Tulsa?

It's not just important to repatriate dollars from individuals who grew up in North Tulsa, have family connections here, or support North Tulsa's revitalization. It is essential to slowly chip away at the misinformation about North Tulsa given to people who live on the south side of the tracks. In many professional circles, the words "North Tulsa" automatically get a negative response. Many of these same people have not stepped a foot in North Tulsa for 20 years or more, and some have never been here at all. A change of perception can only happen if we help others change it. We do this by inviting our co-workers, friends, and members of other communities to events, activities, and neighborhoods in North Tulsa.

I am consistently confused about the views of people because Downtown Tulsa is a booming area, but there are more homeless people walking around those streets than on the streets of North Tulsa. Yet people are willing to go downtown, but not to North Tulsa. Of course, homeless people do not inherently cause hardship to others, but it is interesting that areas with large homeless populations are getting more investments than North Tulsa.

I am in North Tulsa daily or weekly, generally working on some of my real estate investments. I admit that my property has been broken into, and things were stolen. I will also admit I was personally hurt by those incidents because all I want to do is create a better community than the one in which my great-grandmother lived. But despite the existence of thieves in North Tulsa, I also have had my car stolen in East Tulsa, and my cars broken into five times in East Tulsa. We frequently hear on the news about crimes in Midtown, South, and West Tulsa, but those areas continue to snare investments. Even though statistically, North Tulsa is not the most crime-ridden side of town, it is perceived that way.

The North Tulsa Renaissance

As I was picking up the glass from the window, a criminal broke to gain entry into my property; I was reminded that no matter how nice you try to make a community, there would always be people who do not want a better neighborhood because an improving neighborhood may push them out. When people stop hiding behind their curtains and start looking out for one another, we will see a decrease in crime. Some people think they won't get caught, and they have no respect for the property of others. Even with that risk, I still invest because I am working toward a long-term goal, and that is creating sustainable communities and building wealth for my family, friends, and mentors.

We must repatriate the pride of North Tulsa. We must repatriate the sense of community and an "us versus them" mentality against those who would hinder the progress of North Tulsa. The excitement that surrounds the community when something new is created is inspiring, but the shame and disappointment when bad news comes out of North Tulsa can be depressing. If we do not publicize the great works, the new graduates headed to college, the volunteerism, community events, and investments being made, the individuals who no longer live here will only be fed the negative and will remain reluctant to invest in the community.

North Tulsa is ready to be electrified by the works of people who grew up here and invested in the community. North Tulsa can be the blueprint for this type of activity and lead the nation in community building through repatriation. There are businesses that may not work in North Tulsa but would work in South Tulsa. There may also be businesses in South Tulsa that will not work in other parts of the city.

Some businesses cater to the higher-end customer. I'm not saying North Tulsa residents would not be customers at certain price points, but a majority of the customers at the moment are price-point sensitive. When African-Americans started to gain education, financial freedoms, and knowledge about purchasing, the American economy exploded. Some reluctant vendors had to learn how to sell to African-Americans, who now were free people and had money to spend. They wanted the same household items as their white counterparts. They wanted the same cars and the same opportunities to have items crafted that meant something to them personally.

The reason is despite widespread misconceptions, black and white people are the same at their core; they are all people. We are all people first, with common fears, wants, and needs. The community in North Tulsa wants the same cars as people in South Tulsa. They want to stand with pride as their daughters, sons, nieces, and nephews walk across the stage to receive their diplomas. We are more similar than different, but our differences strengthen our similarities.

We see graduates from schools in prominent areas come back and open bars, start tech companies and become teachers in local schools because they believe in their community. They see a future in their community, and they love the place they called home. We have to cultivate and indoctrinate our young people to never forget about what the community has given them, and make them understand they should give the community 100 times what it has given them. I was given incalculable amounts of knowledge, love, and pride from my time growing up in North Tulsa with my great-grandmother, and I want to give back what I received and pay it forward.

The community has a need, and entrepreneurs must feel that need. The community needs the dollars that have left the area to come back in the form of support, investments, and job creation. When our children are graduating from high school and never coming back unless it's on summer vacation, we have a problem. Many universities have alumni organizations with a mission to get the graduates involved with the institution's good works. North Tulsa needs to take that same approach. There could be a database of more than 50,000 people who have ties to North Tulsa but have moved out of the area for various reasons. Some people leave North Tulsa, which is fine, but we don't want the soul of North Tulsa to leave with them.

Just imagine the financial impact if 50,000 people could be set up on a monthly donation to a community development initiative that had the sole purpose of creating change. That financial injection would have a lasting effect on the community. Lives could be saved, jobs could be created, and our community could take its rightful place in Tulsa as a leader in innovation, creativity, and support.

So as a community, what can North Tulsa alumni invest in now? How can someone who is now a successful businessperson in Atlanta but who grew up in North Tulsa invest in the community? The community itself should answer this question. If there are opportunities for that investment and support, let's all get behind them and bring more great things to North Tulsa to build on what we already have. I would love to see young people come together and create the community in which they want to live for years. I would love to see us support their efforts as a community and do our best to ensure they succeed.

The community could partner with the local government to help with the repatriation of North Tulsa alumni dollars. This philosophy or theory is similar to the United States wanting to repatriate dollars that have been sent overseas for tax shelters, and our interest in bringing that money back is so it can be used for development, innovation, job creation, and growth.

The creation of jobs and growth is essential to the success of North Tulsa. The average income lags behind other areas of Tulsa. The high population of not-for-profit organizations limits the sales tax base for the community. North Tulsa is the most prayed-up area in the city due to the over 100 churches in the area. But what comes with being prayed up in the church is the fact that those organizations do not create tax benefits. The churches, although vital, must decide how they will take their rightful role as collective leaders on pushing a message that encourages the repatriation of dollars to North Tulsa. Difficult decisions must also be made about churches that may be hindering investment due to limitations on how far some businesses can be located from a church.

This is not a popular concept, and it is not needed right now. But as the community continues to evolve, this discussion may need to come up more regularly. I would also love to see churches create businesses that are for-profit and help create a sustainable community. The church leaders are charismatic and loved, and many in their flocks would support other business ventures to bring sales and property tax dollars to the community. We need the churches in North Tulsa and we need the prayer, but we also need the attendees of North Tulsa churches to pledge to shop in North Tulsa a couple of times a month.

Imagine the risks of starting a business in the early 1920s, with no support from people who could have been distance cousins and who lived just south of you. That risk is still there for entrepreneurs, but there is more crossing over the North Tulsa line than ever before. Businesses were able to repatriate dollars back into the North Tulsa community and circulate those dollars more than we do today, and they did it with most of their customers looking just like them.

Entrepreneurs now have an opportunity to not only to sell to people who look like them but to others who do not. Our entrepreneurial ancestors did not have that chance, and many died before they were able to see the possibility. Our repatriates have a great opportunity to seize this great opportunity. The history of North Tulsa is already global; now, let's create more global businesses from the community. If successful people who have grown out of North Tulsa had an opportunity to do something great here, I believe they will be willing to take the risk with an investment.

There is a risk of trying to repatriate dollars back into the community. Money leads to corruption, lies, mistrust, and mismanagement, but with the right groups in place, this could be a reality. Risks create rewards, and if O.W. Gurley had not taken a risk, North Tulsa would not have had a Black Wall Street. The next O.W. Gurley may be sitting in class daily in a North Tulsa school. Let's show her that she can be a name for the history books, creating positive change.

What if we were able to bring those dollars back? We could, as they did in the early 1900s, and build our community from the ground up. Entrepreneurs who created the Black Wall Street knew how to repatriate their dollars. Most of their money did not leave the community. This is a different time, but the philosophy is still the same. The formula for success is still the same: Keep your dollars in the community and bring additional dollars to the community.

Those early-day entrepreneurs didn't have the opportunity to bring in additional dollars from other communities. They couldn't get funding from South Tulsa, East Tulsa, or West Tulsa. Also, they didn't have international connections and social media to reach people all over the world. They didn't have vast amounts of resources that are available on the Internet. Our history shows how you bring dollars back to the community and how important it is for certain communities to be self-sustaining and have an additional income and revenue coming from other parts of the city, state, and country.

North Tulsa is in transition, and that transition will be difficult. It's going to require stepping on some toes and ruffling some feathers, but the goal is to see North Tulsa become what the entrepreneurs and leaders in the early 1920s wanted it to become. We need the alumni of North Tulsa to take ownership of this area. Our senior citizens need them, our children need them, and our veterans, single mothers, present fathers, and grandparents need them. And I need them, too.

Suppose the alumni from North Tulsa are able to pool their money and invest in property, as well as resources such as urgent cares, grocery stores, co-working spaces, medical facilities, medical supply facilities, after-school programs, college prep programs, and retail outlets. In that case, the community will forever be grateful and forever be changed. I believe that not only will the community support it, but those outside of the community will also support it.

The North Tulsa Renaissance means supporting your community by opening your community up for others as well. We can no longer sit on the northside of the track. We must show our leadership, dedication, knowledge, and love for the community by putting dollars back into it.

The North Tulsa Repatriation Act does not have to only mean the North Tulsa alumni can pump dollars back into the community. It can also mean North Tulsa is able to gain knowledge from some of the experiences these alumni have accrued. So, if a young boy grows up in North Tulsa, goes to middle school and high school there, then attends college somewhere in the state of Oklahoma and graduates and is a very talented graphic designer now, how do we entice that gentleman to give back to the community?

How do we identify five to 10 companies that could benefit from having a new logo created or having new menus created by one of our North Tulsa alumni? That is how a community is repaid for all the effort, pain, and difficulties it takes to raise a child to be a formidable member of the community. Just think how proud he will be seeing his designs and his original creations sitting on tables his mother sees when she goes to dinner.

Not all investments have dollar figures attached to them. Some investments are repaid by seeing the smile on a single mother's face and the utter glee on the face of a 62-year-old grandmother, and knowing how proud your little brother is of your accomplishments, realizing he has to step up to do the same thing.

Think about a young girl who went to pre-kindergarten, high school, and even college in North Tulsa and has a unique business savvy that allows her to look at an organization from the bottom up and identify its needs and the wants of her customers. Imagine if that North Tulsa alumni, who may not have $3,000 to invest right now, could help a nonprofit organization struggling with funding or with identifying which programs work best for the community. That young lady can now make a change so that organization will be able to help thousands of people inside and outside of her community. That's the importance of repatriating dollars and talents back to North Tulsa.

Imagine a young boy who had some difficulties in elementary school, struggled through high school in North Tulsa and had to go to a junior college, even though he has D-1 college talents in soccer because his grades weren't good enough to qualify him for a major university. After completing his two years in junior college, he now qualifies to go to a university. Upon entering the university, the young man finds a mentor who refuses to allow him to become a statistic. That mentor sees potential in this young man, and he knows if that young man goes back home, he will die, wind up in prison or forever work low-income jobs. That mentor is now repatriating his service to this young man because he is investing in the North Tulsa revitalization. The youth of North Tulsa is our investment. The mentor wants to see this young man do well and be able to take care of his mother and aging father. So, he invests his time, knowledge, dedication, and toughness into this young investment.

Let's say this young man becomes extremely active in college. He joins political organizations, volunteers in the community and thinks he's found his calling. This young man now wants to graduate and lead other young people. He wants to be an educator and an administrator so he can help people like his mentor helped him. This young man now wants to go back to North Tulsa and become a leader in the education field. He aspires to be a principal and then move up to the school board because he wants to see a change. He wants to invest back into his community the way his mentor did for him. That's a return on investment North Tulsa needs. This young investment will now mentor and inspire hundreds, if not thousands, of people. There is no better return on investment than that.

You don't have to live in North Tulsa to invest in North Tulsa. Invest in our children's future, invest in our communities, and see your investment grow and inspire others. We complain that we don't have a fair shake in this world and that we see development happening in other areas of the city, but not in North Tulsa. But are those areas doing a better job of repatriating their young people who want to

The North Tulsa Renaissance

come back to their town and educate, volunteer, protect, and lead their communities? The development we see in Downtown Tulsa, in South Tulsa, and now even in West Tulsa, started with a vision and a risk that many in North Tulsa have not been willing to take. It will take someone or a group of people to risk thousands upon thousands of dollars on their ideology, on their idea of a better community.

Are you ready to take that risk? Can you convince your North Tulsa alumni to take the risk with you so you can realize the North Tulsa Renaissance? People must be willing to lose money, political capital, and community support to even think about large investments in North Tulsa. The organizations investing in Downtown Tulsa and South Tulsa do it for a reason. They see a return on their investment, and they see a benefit to investing in those areas. They feel the people will appreciate, support, assist in monitoring the properties, and provide safe living quarters in those areas. This is a key change that must happen to realize the North Tulsa Renaissance.

We all want to see a better Tulsa, but so many forget that North Tulsa is key to a better Tulsa. North Tulsans leave their communities daily to make South Tulsa and Downtown Tulsa better places. This is the same approach that was used in 1921. North Tulsans have left their community to prop up, lead, support, and invest in communities and organizations south of their own homes.

During the height of the Black Wall Street, North Tulsa entrepreneurs could not count on the support of South Tulsa patrons, but 100 years later, North Tulsa entrepreneurs need the support of South Tulsa patrons. They need them to help take their businesses to the next level. They also need support from other cities and states to expand their businesses. The core support starts in North Tulsa, but the expansion of support from South Tulsa is paramount for some of the businesses in North Tulsa.

You must not shut off a potential moneymaking opportunity because you want only support from your own community. If you do, you will not survive and thrive as you should. It's not accepting a handout but expanding your influence. That is how Downtown Tulsa and South Tulsa have expanded into North Tulsa – not by investing in North Tulsa, but by showing North Tulsans they have the goods they want. North Tulsa entrepreneurs must do the same.

The question is, do you offer a good or service they do not already have in Downtown or South Tulsa? The likelihood of that is small, but you can offer better service, a different way of providing that service, or a hyper-local experience instead of a corporate experience. I feel more North Tulsa residents will begin to realize that to expand North Tulsa, we must be an open North Tulsa. We are open for business. Come shop with us!

As we repatriate groups of people, we will always have additional groups of people who want to get involved. There will always be people graduating or who had relatives who lived in North Tulsa and now are doing very well for themselves. There will be people who will see investments and developments happening in North Tulsa and want to get in on the action. How do we reach them?

The North Tulsa Renaissance

I often hear that development will raise housing and rent prices, which will push people out of the community. I am always battled by that belief. Do you want a better community, or do you want the status quo? In order to break the generational poverty cycle, we must give people a reason to want to do better. If they know their community no longer wants to accept living the low-income life, they may do things in their lives to help them afford to ride the wave of increased prices. With investment comes improvement; with improvement comes development; with development comes better housing, and with housing comes opportunities for early investment in buying a home in North Tulsa that will increase in value. That is why it is vital that North Tulsans buy and develop the abundant housing they have in the community. Invest early, and you will benefit from the increase in property value. Don't allow yourself to become a victim of being priced out of the market. Be a benefactor of the market. Decide to be a part of the people who see housing prices rising in North Tulsa so you can reap the benefits.

I want the kids in elementary school to see their mothers' own homes within their lifetimes. I want kids in high school to see their mothers work to obtain a degree or certification within their lifetimes, and I want to see kids in college able to come back to North Tulsa to live in an area of town in which they want to invest their money and talents. No longer will we sit on the sidelines and complain about what is being done to us. We will be at the table if we demand our right to be valued, listened to, invested with, and supported as other parts of Tulsa.

Chapter 20
The Grand Finale

As I try to describe my view of the North Tulsa Renaissance, I think about all the small children, who only dream of being better and enjoy their lives. I think about all the children who would never succeed because of the community or situations they live in. I think about the children who would never walk on a college campus, realize their dream to become an author or an entrepreneur, and I get worried.

My job on this earth is to create and teach, and it all starts with our children. If our community is to have the Renaissance it deserves, our children must understand the principles earlier children understood when our community was thriving. That meant having respect for themselves: how they look, smell, and dress, how they speak, what they put in their heads – and respect for others, especially their elders.

Our grandmothers and grandfathers were more active. They were older as well, and children in those days understood respect. We must pursue that ideal in our community to help save our children. It's vital to a North Tulsa Renaissance that we respect our elderly and do everything we can to help take care of them and make sure they have the resources they need to live. We must support the new visions of North Tulsa.

We must not isolate ourselves from other communities but must instead integrate our ideas and plans. We can learn from others who have built up their communities and use their resources to create thriving neighborhoods. South Tulsa and Downtown Tulsa are vibrant communities. They have been able to benefit from services, funding, knowledge, and research, and we must tap into these things to build the North Tulsa Renaissance.

It is important for the community to create sustainable entrepreneurs. Owners of land and businesses built North Tulsa, and their recipes for success are still valid to this day. Our community must invest in property and push our children into technology, science, mathematics, law, public safety, city planning, entrepreneurship, and the medical field. These are critical areas that will help the North Tulsa community for years to come. We must produce more college and tech school graduates. And we must help more single parents go back to school and get an education.

North Tulsa has a vast amount of undeveloped land that is primed for new retail and new ideas. There are empty lots in almost every neighborhood in North Tulsa. We need a plan for those empty lots. How do we use our land to create sustainable neighborhoods? Do we build tiny homes on those lots, or do we create mixed neighborhoods where we have a form of retail within the neighborhoods? Can the land be used to create gardens, storage units, daycares, police and public safety checks, or other essential services?

The North Tulsa Renaissance

We as a people have a unique opportunity in front of us. The land is cheap and is waiting for great ideas to develop it. This land has been available for years, and before developers come in from outside the community, we should pull our money together to purchase the land and develop it. We have a chance to create the community we want. Will you be one of those who will do it?

If city leaders see that we're serious, they'll help support our plans, but we must support their ideas as well, or at least be there to listen to them. If we disagree, we must voice our concerns in a respectful way. But we can't just care about our own community; we must care about Tulsa as a whole. If there are council meetings focusing on South Tulsa or Downtown Tulsa, we must be at those meetings because what we can learn there is vital to our enhanced knowledge of government dealings. Whenever we only go to committee meetings in large numbers when they affect our community, we lose power because officials will think we only care about our community rather than Tulsa as a whole.

If North Tulsa is to evolve into a viable community, we must change the stigma attached to it. That starts with North Tulsans themselves, who are some of the proudest people in the country. We must harness that attitude and turn it into action. We must take it to the streets and gather support from the community on key initiatives. We must stand up to violence and refuse to tolerate our little children getting killed by people who look just like them. We must stand up to drug dealers and bad landlords who leave houses condemned for years and years, where our single mothers and elderly are forced to live. We must start building up our

The North Tulsa Renaissance

community by cleaning up our neighborhoods. Cutting the grass and cleaning up trash on the streets make the community look presentable.

The city government must be involved in rebranding North Tulsa. Officials must get more involved in the community to showcase the great things going on in North Tulsa. The city of Tulsa just announced a $100 million project to build up a certain area in Downtown Tulsa. In previous years, Downtown Tulsa was an undesirable place for entertainment, but local government and the private sector partnered, and now the area looks amazing. Why is that effort not put into North Tulsa? There are areas that could be turned into entertainment districts, but those areas lie fallow. It is no one person's fault, but one person could start the change. Who is that one person who will eventually turn into a group of people to partner with the local government and the private sector to launch entertainment initiatives in North Tulsa? That person could be you and your circle of friends.

The years and years of effective negative marketing against North Tulsa and its residents have done its job. Now it's not just the people outside of the community who believe it; the destructive views of others have convinced some in the community. All communities deal with some form of undesirable activity, whether it's domestic or gang violence, robbery, bribery, or drugs. But some of those communities still thrive. We must ensure that North Tulsa does the same.

North Tulsa is ready for investment. Its population is ready for new training for employment opportunities. North Tulsa is primed and ready for major investment in the education system that will help decrease the dropout rate and increase the drop-in rate on college campuses. The community has not been without its challenges and missed opportunities, but we can complain about that for another 100 years, or we can take calculated steps to make history. There is no reason that North Tulsa cannot have the same or more amenities than it had in the early 1900s. If it doesn't happen, that's a tragedy.

Many would blame the race massacre for 100 years of missed opportunity, unrealized investments, and substandard educational standards. To those and everyone else, I offer hope that our ancestors who built Black Wall Street were recent descendants of slavery who refused to blame their circumstances because back then, they did not even have the same opportunities we have now. Excuses did not build South Tulsa, and it will not build North Tulsa. Hope, planning, passion, support, investments, and education will do that. Doubt does not pour one block of concrete; it does not swipe one credit card of the first customer at a new shop, and it does not offer a path forward.

Many areas in North Tulsa are safe and ready for investment and new ideas. We must support entrepreneurship and development by holding their feet to the fire and making sure they're going to provide excellent customer service, quality products, and give back to the community. Some of the companies' profits should stay in the community that supports them. We have seen a casino rake in millions of dollars from North Tulsa residents, only to take those profits, build a new casino and tear down the old one. What's worse, they took it upon themselves to call

The North Tulsa Renaissance

their North Tulsa casino a "Downtown Casino." Just imagine the effect on a community to see a multimillion-dollar business support the community from which it gleans most of its profits! When will corporations take pride in being based in North Tulsa? Why do they not want to be associated with North Tulsa? As we take an internal autopsy about North Tulsa, we must ask ourselves that question. North Tulsans have pride, but do the companies have a similar pride?

North Tulsa houses some of our city's best family attractions, largest manufacturing locations, and substantial higher education presence, but a casual observer would think that is not the case because of the way the community is perceived. Our current generation can change that, and it must do so, or it may take another 100 years to bring any development to fruition.

Community health, education, safety, real estate investments, entrepreneurship, and innovation will be the keys to the North Tulsa Renaissance, and support for initiatives, projects, and development is essential to the change that is coming to North Tulsa. We must hold all those who want to bring development to the community to maintain the same standards they held in South Tulsa. We must no longer allow them to take money out of our community and invest it in other areas without investing in North Tulsa schools, infrastructure, music and art programs, and sports programs. No longer must we sit idly by and just complain. We shall become the "we do" community. We will show the world what we can do, what we will do, and what we will not do. This will be a great generation to become change agents and advocates for change.

Change is difficult and even scary, but we have to start rebuilding our community. This is easy to say but challenging to accomplish. People will have to take a risk on the community to see the long-term gains financially and socially. In the 1920s, entrepreneurs created their businesses not to get rich but to survive. Gaining financial independence does not happen with one project; it happens by establishing multiple streams of income, and North Tulsa allows for that. A young millionaire could be created by simply generating solutions to problems that organizations and companies deal with in North Tulsa. Those solutions could be implemented in other areas of the city and the country. Our young people have the energy, blind ambition, and technological expertise to come up with solutions. We just need more adults to put them in places of influence so they can gain the knowledge, skills, and abilities needed to elevate them to their full potential.

A question that is frequently asked is, "When will we see big-box chains come to North Tulsa?" My answer is, "When the community looks profitable." Many, if not most multicity or multistate companies started with one location that garnered enough support to expand to more locations. That is why support is essential. North Tulsa's companies can become the starting point for businesses that will expand to other cities and states. Success for our entrepreneurs means success for the community as a whole. It is also a success for our ancestors and for our own future.

The North Tulsa Renaissance

Small businesses drive our country's investments, employment, and innovation, so it is incumbent upon us to support our small businesses and our local companies to help them become viable and profitable. The innovators, visionaries, and supporters from the early 1900s knew they had to rely on their own communities to save them. They knew they had to educate their children and hold the administrators of those schools accountable for higher graduation rates. We can find pictures showing poor children who were dressed for school the same way they dressed for church. They did not have new shoes or clothing, but they had their books in their hands and were ready to learn and better themselves.

Our community must hold the politicians, principals, counselors, and teachers of our schools to a high standard. The community must hold our parents to a higher standard to ensure their children are being educated. We must stamp out generational poverty by supporting single mothers and insisting that estranged fathers take their rightful roles as partners in raising their children. Government assistance should not be the de facto fathers and supporters of our children anymore. Absent fathers must step up and help their children. Parents should put differences aside for the good of the children. It is their duty to insert themselves into the lives of their children and let the grandparents know they appreciate everything they've done to help support the single mother as she raises the children. It's time for absent fathers to pay back the grandparents for their investment in the children while those fathers were not there. They can pay them back simply by being present.

Our protest should not be limited to police officers killing, profiling, or harassing black people. Our greatest risk to our children is to allow them to become adults encumbered by the very things we do not protest. We do not protest failing schools, drugs, and murders in our very own community, and we do not protest and hold accountable those who have helped harm our community. We can no longer allow ourselves to be pushed over and pushed around. Although real oppression does occur in this country, we must stamp out the way we oppress our own communities.

My mother always told me you teach people how to treat you. If we treat our elderly, veterans, single mothers, present fathers, and children with respect, others will also have that respect. If we teach our children how to show and demand respect, others will respect them. If we teach our children the importance of volunteering, others will invite them to learn about their organizations via internships that could turn into permanent jobs and even entrepreneurship opportunities.

The local government has a role to play in the North Tulsa Renaissance. Few developments or projects are initiated in Tulsa without government involvement by inspections, joint partnerships, tax incentives, and land sales. The reluctance of the city government to invest in North Tulsa is eye-opening. If the local government who takes in our tax dollars does not see the community as a worthy investment, how will outside investors see it? There must be a positive perception of North Tulsa and coordination with the local government to reinvest in the area.

The North Tulsa Renaissance

Not only should we push the importance of college to our youth, but we must also advocate trade school options for our high school students. Image a young adult with a business degree and trade school training. That student may end up making more money in the future than those with master's degrees because not only will they know how to bid for an electrical, plumbing, or HVAC job, they will know how to manage their own businesses. For young adults who do not desire to go to college, trade programs can be the key to financial success. As a real estate investor, I have paid contractors more than I have earned from certain projects, so I know that learning trades is extremely important. Not many jobs will allow an individual to bid $5,000 for work to be completed within three weeks. Imagine one tradesperson having three or four of those projects going at one time! Those bids are available in North Tulsa right now. That is financial freedom.

People in the community must no longer accept the attitude of residents in South, West, and East Tulsa that North Tulsa is the most dangerous part of town. We must no longer allow new businesses to come into North Tulsa or to bid on a project if the owners believe our residents are not worth the investment. We must sell North Tulsa instead of putting it on a slab for an autopsy. That's how we make a great community.

The American dream of homeownership is attainable in North Tulsa. The inventory of empty houses is plentiful and affordable. Some will rent a majority of their lives, but there is such a great opportunity to own real estate in North Tulsa that can be passed down to loved ones or eventually generate income as rentals. The local housing authority helps interested members of the community learn more about homeownership, pay toward their closing costs, and help set them up for financial freedom in the future.

It is better to pay yourself rather than to pay for another person's mortgage. Paying rent does not put money in your pocket, and it doesn't create equity. Instead, it puts a small amount of money into the landlord's pockets. Why not put that money into your pockets in the form of paying down an asset that you will own one day? As a landlord, I understand the need of many people to rent, but I advocate homeownership whenever possible because it can mean the difference between poverty and financial independence. Even if you have to buy a small house that is less than desirable, it will be yours, and you can slowly fix it up. Paint is inexpensive but can change an entire house. You can also work on one home improvement per paycheck or with each tax return received. Those in affluent parts of town have higher rates of homeownership, which increases their net worth, permits, tax deductions and allows them to leave assets to their children rather than lease applications.

The paradigm of North Tulsa must continue to shift. There are great organizations, supporters, entrepreneurs, educators, public safety officers, and leaders in North Tulsa, and we must continue to build on their visions, initiatives, and ideas. The great people of North Tulsa are laying the groundwork for a better North Tulsa. The large-scale corporations investing in North Tulsa may not be as widely known, but they see value in locating in the community. We must invite them to stay involved from a social and financial standpoint.

The youth are the impetus for a vibrant North Tulsa. Without their future repatriation, the community will lose a valuable pipeline of innovators. The elders have seen it all except for a vibrant North Tulsa, as it was envisioned in the early 1900s. Let's show them that their life-long support, sacrifice, and determination have not been for naught.

Those outside of the community should get ready to visit and support North Tulsa because with its resurgence will come a national spotlight on Tulsa's greatness as a whole. No longer should those who live outside of North Tulsa allow what others say in a negative way to affect their opinion. They must be encouraged to visit a church service, a library, or a sporting event, eat at a restaurant, attend a parade or a Juneteenth celebration, or just walk around and take in the air. North Tulsa has a lot to offer Tulsa as a whole, and we must remember all the contributions North Tulsans make to the overall Tulsa economy.

The North Tulsa Renaissance starts with you. Let's spread love, not hate.

www.ingramcontent.com/pod-product-compliance
Lightning Source LLC
Chambersburg PA
CBHW050117280326
41933CB00010B/1141